Freedom and Recognition in the Work of Simone de Beauvoir

Philosophy, Phenomenology and Hermeneutics of Values
Philosophie, Phänomenologie und Hermeneutik der Werte
Philosophie, Phénoménologie et Herméneutique des Valeurs

Book series of the Institute for Axiological Research
General Editor: Yvanka B. Raynova

Vol. 3

PETER LANG
Frankfurt am Main · Berlin · Bern · Bruxelles · New York · Oxford · Wien

Susanne Moser

Freedom and Recognition in the Work of Simone de Beauvoir

PETER LANG
Internationaler Verlag der Wissenschaften

Bibliographic Information published by the Deutsche Nationalbibliothek
The Deutsche Nationalbibliothek lists this publication in the Deutsche Nationalbibliografie; detailed bibliographic data is available in the internet at <http://www.d-nb.de>.

Supported by the City of Vienna, Cultural Department –
Science and Research Promotion

The translation was made possible by the
Austrian Federal Ministry of Science and Research

Printed with the support of the
Austrian Federal Ministry of Science and Research

Cover image:
male / female, 1994 by Susanne Moser
© Susanne Moser

ISSN 1611-258X
ISBN 978-3-631-50925-8
© Peter Lang GmbH
Internationaler Verlag der Wissenschaften
Frankfurt am Main 2008
All rights reserved.

All parts of this publication are protected by copyright. Any utilisation outside the strict limits of the copyright law, without the permission of the publisher, is forbidden and liable to prosecution. This applies in particular to reproductions, translations, microfilming, and storage and processing in electronic retrieval systems.

Printed in Germany 1 2   4 5 6 7

www.peterlang.de

For Yvanka B. Raynova

Contents

Introductory Remarks 9
On the Reception of Beauvoir's Work 17

Part I
Ambiguity, Freedom, Morality

Pyrrhus et Cinéas 38
   The Project 41
   The Justification of Existence 51
The Ethics of Ambiguity 59
   Freedom and Finitude 62
   Death 62
   The Concept of Ambiguity 66
Freedom and Transcendence 74
   The Ontological Dimension of Freedom 74
   The Liberation to Freedom: the Ethical Dimension of
   Transcendence in the Work of Simone de Beauvoir 87
   Freedom as a Developmental Process:
   The Problem of childhood 95
   Being and Failure 103

Part II
Subject, Society, Recognition

Recognition between Conflict and Reciprocity 111
   She Came to Stay 114
   Recognition – Subject – Transcendence: Conceptual and
   Methodological Foundations of *The Second Sex* 124
   The Social Dimension of Transcendence 126

The Concept of the Subject 129
　　The Subject of Existence 130
　　The Subject of Morality 134
　　The Subject of Dominance 136
The Concept of Recognition 140
　　The Master-Slave Dialectics in *The Second Sex* 142
　　The Myth of Femininity 152
　　Mutual Recognition: Friendship 158
The Woman as Subject 162
　　The Question of Woman 168
　　Situation 171
　　The Body 177
　　Identity 188
　　Existence 193
Paths to Liberation 197

Bibliography 214

Introductory Remarks

"Enough ink has been spilled in quarreling over feminism, now practically over, and perhaps we should say no more about it. It is still talked about, however, for the voluminous nonsense uttered during the last century seems to have done little to illuminate the problem."[1] This sentence does not originate from a recent discussion, but was chosen as the opening line in *The Second Sex* by Simone de Beauvoir, so as to point out from the beginning the ever-present assumption that the problem with the woman's place in society has already been solved. Instead, according to Beauvoir, there remains only confusion. If we are to gain understanding, we should get out of these ruts; we should discard the vague notions of superiority, inferiority and equality which have hitherto corrupted every discussion of the subject and start afresh.[2]

More than fifty years later, we find ourselves at a similar point. Why do we need any more feminist theories if everything has been said already? In this regard, writing a book about Simone de Beauvoir could seem quite superfluous. Against her intentions Beauvoir's approach was shelved as equality feminism, and many feminists of our present time consider her to be outmoded, "historical heritage" at best.

---

[1] Simone de Beauvoir, *The Second Sex*, New York: Vintage Books Edition, 1989, p. 19.
[2] Ibidem, p. 23.

Why therefore should a new book surface about the work of Simone de Beauvoir, why now an English version of the German original[3]?

The book at hand for the first time offers a detailed introduction into Beauvoir's philosophy where the focus is on her concepts of freedom and recognition and their impact on a philosophy of gender. At the same time the importance of philosophy for feminist theory as a whole will be emphasized. It will be shown that Beauvoir is much more than a simple equality feminist and that she posed questions that are nowadays at the center of feminist interest. At the beginning of the book a short chapter will deal with the reception of Beauvoir's work in the English-speaking scientific community as regards discussions relevant in our context.

The feminist theorists of difference reproach Beauvoir for equating being human with masculinity, for espousing a theory of equality, and for depreciating being a woman. In the period of feminist theory which followed, the subject of feminism itself, namely being a woman, was questioned. During the conflicts which then arose between essentialism and constructivism Beauvoir's work remained unnoticed because it was identified solely with the feminist theory of equality. Both positions are being regarded here as insufficient, and the thesis is evolved that it was not on any account Beauvoir's intention to create a model of equality, but also to pose the question of difference. Which ethical, social and cultural consequences would have to be drawn

---

[3] Susanne Moser, *Freiheit und Anerkennung bei Simone de Beauvoir*, Tübingern: edition discord, 2002.
As regards the English version I owe thanks to Michael Harlan Lyman for his ambitious draft translation and to Rebecca White as an expert proof-reader.

so that the "new woman" could finally manifest herself? The woman would have to shed her old skin, writes Beauvoir in *The Second Sex*, and "cut her own new clothes".[4] To emancipate woman would mean to refuse to confine her to the relations she bears to man and to offer her the possibility to posit herself independently.[5] This question of Beauvoir corresponds to the endeavors of the theories of feminist difference, namely to understand femininity in a positive way. But, whereas feminist theories of difference take an unambiguous female identity for granted, linked to the female body, Beauvoir links being a woman to the ambiguity of existence. Similarly, as in post-modern feminism, existentialism rejects any fixed pre-assigned identity.

Beauvoir emphasizes that, independent of how important contributions of biology, psychoanalysis, and historical materialism might be, "we shall hold that the body, the sexual life, and the resources of technology exist concretely for man only in so far as he grasps them in the total perspective of his existence."[6] In the following, it will be demonstrated that Beauvoir approaches the problem of existence on three different levels: on the level of the situation, of the body and of the identity, which however must not be considered separately. The body is interlinked directly with existence, it is a synthetic unity, that itself is to be understood only through the situation, its relation to the world, whereby the situation is not something given but reveals itself only in the act of existence. Beauvoir emphasizes that for the human being nature has reality only to the extent that it is in-

---

[4] Simone de Beauvoir, *The Second Sex*, p. 725.
[5] Ibidem, p. 731.
[6] Ibidem, p. 60.

volved in his activity – his own nature not excepted.[7] "In truth, however, the nature of things is no more immutably given, once for all, than is historical reality."[8] She does not even regard sexual difference as a necessary attribute to existence, it seems conceivable to her that "the perpetuation of the species does not necessitate sexual differentiation (...) we can imagine a parthenogenetic or hermaphroditic society."[9] But also with regard to the transgender debate, Beauvoir's approach creates stimulus. Gender is not only something constructed, something that one is *for* others and *through* others – as it is assumed in most sociological theories of gender construction – but is also connected to one's self-perception. So Beauvoir speaks explicitly of the woman being a female only to the extent to which "she feels herself as such (...) It is not nature that defines woman; it is she who defines herself by dealing with nature on her own account in her emotional life."[10]

Our studies rest on the assumption that Beauvoir's existentialist approach must be taken seriously, in that it provides the basis for the analysis of gender relations. Therefore connections to Sartre are being established in order to show where Beauvoir is in accordance or in opposition to his philosophy, and to expel existing prejudices, for example that his *for-itself* represents a body-less and position-less absolute freedom. Additionally it is demonstrated that Beauvoir, contrary to Sartre, derives freedom not only from transcendence, but also from will. Beauvoir is defining the

---

[7] Ibidem, p. 35.
[8] Ibidem, p. 60.
[9] Ibidem, p. 7.
[10] Ibidem, p. 38.

notion of ambiguity not only in dependence on Sartre, but also in connection with Hegel. The human being tries to escape from his natural condition without, however, being able to freeing himself from it.[11] Beauvoir emphasizes that the fundamental ambiguity of the human being must not be concealed, or as in Hegel's work, surpassed on a higher level, yet as will be shown in the course of this study in certain places Beauvoir adheres to this very idea. Modernity devaluates all processes that happen by nature without free creation by the human being as a stage that needs to be overcome and mastered. Repeatedly, Beauvoir places the overcoming of life, where you "take control of the instant and mold the future"[12], in contrast to a life of animalistic nature. By way of analogy she devalues the work connected with reproduction mostly performed by women.

One of the goals of this book is to point out the conflicts in which Beauvoir is involved by making use of the emancipation potential of classical German philosophy, especially Hegel. Building on this philosophical tradition of liberation she criticizes its misogynic tendency and yet partly falls victim to it herself. For instance she will maintain throughout her life that one should not orient oneself on female values. Believing in female values would imply a belief in female nature, something she had always fought against.[13] Regrettably, she does not arrive at the same conclusion when referring to male values: instead of questioning them in the same way using the existentialist and de-

---

[11] Simone de Beauvoir, *The Ethics of Ambiguity,* Secaucus, N. J.: Citadel Press Book, Carol Publishing Group Edition 1997, p. 7.
[12] Ibidem, p. 65.
[13] Alice Schwarzer, *Simone de Beauvoir. Rebellin und Wegbereiterin,* Köln: Kiepenheuer & Witsch 1999, p. 58.

constructivistic approach, they are still approved of and taken for granted by her as a general point of reference. Using her work, also the conflicts are shown that arise when modern emancipation discourse and post-modern deconstructivism clash. In a detailed study of these conflicting tendencies the thesis is elaborated that Beauvoir's work can be seen as a pivot between modernity and postmodernity.

The structure of the book follows the development of Beauvoir's work from her earlier writings up to *The Second Sex* also including her late study on *Old Age* and her autobiographies. Beginning with *Pyrrhus et Cinéas*[14] it will be shown how Beauvoir investigates the meaning of projects, and the need to justify existence. Only the concrete realization of one's projects, not a pre-assigned order from birth onward, can determine one's place in the world. To reduce a human being to his/her[15] status acquired by birth is for Beauvoir not only an anachronism, but also the highest form of suppression because here a decrease of transcendence into immanence takes place. Beauvoir herself claims to point out generally valid suppression mechanisms against women of all cultural backgrounds and of all eras. This general claim will be rejected in this study and the thesis is supported that Beauvoir's concept of the woman as the "Absolute Other" reflects the exclusion mechanisms specific to modernity. Beauvoir appears to be a precursor of post-modern justice theories, by pointing out the subtle ex-

---

[14] Simone de Beauvoir, *Pyrrhus et Cinéas*, Paris: Gallimard 1944 (no English translation available).
[15] We use this politically correct solution in our text, but have refrained from rewording quotations in that respect.

clusion mechanisms produced by certain myths and simulacra as well as by fixed qualities ascribed to women thereby preventing them from taking part in the process of recognition.[16]

50 years on from the publication of *The Second Sex* these exclusion mechanisms can no longer halt the emancipation of women in terms of legal equality and participation in public life. But as long as life projects differ, depending on whether one is in charge of reproductive work or not, and as long as the ascription of this duty is linked to a certain gender construction, these subtle exclusion mechanisms will still prevail. In light of this there can never be enough said or written about all these problems.

---

[16] See: Yvanka B. Raynova. "Für eine postmoderne Ethik der Gerechtigkeit: Simone de Beauvoir und Jean-François Lyotard, in: Yvanka B. Raynova, Susanne Moser (eds.), *Simone de Beauvoir. 50 Jahre nach dem anderen Geschlecht*, Frankfurt am Main: Peter Lang Verlag 2004, p. 141-155. At this point I would like to extend my special thanks to my colleague Yvanka B. Raynova, phenomenologist, expert on Sartre and translator of his works into Bulgarian, for her critical reading, advice and encouragement when I was writing the book at hand.

On the Reception of Beauvoir's Work

After its publication in 1949, *The Second Sex* caused a scandal[17] and was ardently discussed, but its largest effect was to reveal itself later. By the end of the sixties, *The Second Sex* had turned into the Bible of the Women's Liberation Movement. In Europe and the USA women-self-awareness groups formed, in which *The Second Sex* was read and discussed, not as a theoretical work but in connection with personal experiences. But vehement resistance soon motioned and created a growing gap between the Women's Liberation Movement, its Bible and its mother.[18] Within the developing feminist theories increasing reservation was expressed against Beauvoir's theoretical approach. Therefore the discussion of Beauvoir's work must be viewed in connection and in interaction with the different phases of feminist theory. Closely connected is the question of the importance accorded to philosophy in feminist theories, either accusing philosophy of male thinking and rejecting it altogether or trying to position it in a new way.

---

[17] Beauvoir writes in her memoirs *Force of Circumstance*, that after the publishing of *The Second Sex* she had been reproached of being "unsatisfied, frigid, priapic, nymphomaniac, lesbian, a hundred times aborted, I was everything, even an unmarried mother." Mauriac had written to one of the staff members of *Les Temps Modernes*: "Your employer's vagina has no secrets from me," He began a series in *Le Figaro Littéraire* urging the youth of France to condemn pornography in general and Beauvoir's articles in particular. Its success had been slight. Simone de Beauvoir, *Force of Circumstance*, Harmondsworth: Pinguin Books 1968, p. 197.

[18] Jo-Ann Pilardi, *Feminists Read The Second Sex*, in: Margaret A. Simons (ed.), *Feminist Interpretations of Simone de Beauvoir*, University Park: The Pennsylvania State University Press, 1995, p. 31.

We must also take into account that it was difficult for Beauvoir's work to be acknowledged within academic circles, since it was more prestigious to write about a male author than a female one.[19]

For a long while it was Beauvoir's personal life and her relation to Sartre which was a point of interest, as opposed to her work. *The Second Sex* was not considered as a philosophical work, but as a sociological one, and as the companion of Sartre, Beauvoir was seen to be simply applying his existential philosophy. Also Beauvoir regarded herself more as an author of novels than a philosopher, thus contributing herself to the fact that her philosophical questions were not seriously discussed for a long time.

Hazel Barnes, translator of Sartre's *Being and Nothingness*, saw in Beauvoir's novel *She Came to Stay*, an illustration of Sartre's *Being and Nothingness*. One is virtually able to sense, Hazel Barnes wrote, how much Beauvoir had been carried by the inspiration to elaborate Sartre's abstract principles into real life. However, according to Barnes, it cannot be ruled out that Beauvoir might have contributed a lot to Sartre's philosophy, and that he may be immensely indebted to her. Barnes however wanted to show that the novel had served as documentation for Sartre's theory, independent of who may have had which idea first.[20]

These questions also preoccupied Margaret A. Simons right from the onset of her Beauvoir research in 1969: not only did she want to prove Beauvoir's philosophical auton-

---

[19] See: Elizabeth Fallaize (ed.), *Simone de Beauvoir: A Critical Reader*, London/New York: Routledge 1998, p. 7 and p. 132.
[20] Hazel Barnes, *Self-Encounter in She Came to Stay*, in: Elizabeth Fallaize (ed.), *Simone de Beauvoir. A Critical Reader*, London/New York: Routledge 1998, p. 157, see also footnote 1 on page 170.

omy in relation to Sartre, but additionally she wanted to point out the large philosophical influence Beauvoir had on Sartre's philosophy. In her book of 1999 she even claims that Beauvoir had already anticipated the philosophy of existentialism in her early diaries.[21] Since these diaries were not accessible before 1990, it took her almost 30 years to substantiate her early suppositions.[22] Also Kate and Edward Fullbrook had to wait for the publication of Sartre's *War Diaries* and Beauvoir's *Letters to Sartre* in order to be able to present the relationship of Sartre and Beauvoir in a new light.[23] The Fullbrooks developed the theory that Beauvoir not only had a large influence on Sartre's work, but that Beauvoir had formulated her own philosophical system before Sartre, which he then adopted and presented as his own.[24] Regardless of the extent to which we can fol-

---

[21] Margaret A. Simons, *Beauvoir and The Second Sex. Feminism, Race, and the Origins of Existentialism*, Boston: Rowman & Littlefield 1999, see especially the preface.

[22] In 1986 Sylvie Le Bon de Beauvoir, adopted daughter of Simone de Beauvoir, found Beauvoir's handwritten *Carnets de Jeunesse*. In 1990 she gave them to the national library, where Margaret A. Simons could study them. See: Margaret A. Simons, *Beauvoir's Early Philosophy: The 1927 Diary*. In: Margaret A. Simons, *Beauvoir and The Second Sex*, Rowman&Littlefield, Boston 1999, p. 185-245; see also: Margaret A. Simons, *The Beginnings of Beauvoir's Existential Phenomenology*, in: Wendy O'Brien and Lester Embree (ed.), *The Existential Phenomenology of Simone de Beauvoir*, Dordrecht/Boston/London: Kluwer Academic Publishers 2001, p. 17-40.

[23] Kate and Edward Fullbrook, *Simone de Beauvoir and Jean-Paul Sartre: The Remaking of a Twentieth-Century Legend*, New York: Basic Books 1994.

[24] Kate Fullbrook and Edward Fullbrook, *Sartre's Secret Key*, in: Margaret A. Simons (ed.), *Feminist Interpretations of Simone de Beauvoir*, University Park: The Pennsylvania State University Press 1995, p. 108.

low these assumptions, since the 1990s it has certainly not been possible any more to regard Beauvoir as Sartre's student, as was still the case in *Le petit Larousse* of 1974.[25]

In 1990 Margaret A. Simons together with Azizah Y. Al-Hibri published in *Hypatia Reborn*[26] a Beauvoir-focus, compiled predominantly of contributions to a philosophical conference held in 1984, named *The Second Sex: A New Beginning*.[27] In contrast to the conventional opinion, that regarded *The Second Sex* as antiquated, outdated, determined by male thinking and as sheer application of Sartre's philosophy, Simons not only emphasized the importance of *The Second Sex* as the point of origin for feminist theory, but regarded it as the basis of feminist philosophy in general and the basis for every further philosophical differentiation. Yet, Simons stresses that in the course of time something like a negative defense against the big mother had developed in feminist consciousness: "'Who I am' began with 'How I'm not like her'."[28]

However the unification of such different approaches as feminism and philosophy to feminist philosophy incurred difficulties. The claim of feminism and the Women's Liberation Movement to judge everything directly from one's own experience and to also benefit from it was incorporated into feminist philosophy and resulted in a contradic-

---

[25] See also: Toril Moi, *Simone de Beauvoir. The Making of an Intellectual Woman,* Cambridge MA: Blackwell 1994, p. 15.

[26] *Hypatia Reborn* is the first number of the new edition of the journal *Hypatia: A Journal of Feminist Philosophy.*

[27] Azizah Y. Al-Hibri and Margaret A. Simons (eds.), *Hypatia Reborn. Essays in Feminist Philosophy*, Bloomington: Indiana University Press 1990.

[28] Ibidem, p. 227.

tion with the claim of philosophy to be objective and universally valid. So the question arose as to whether *The Second Sex* could be regarded as a feminist work at all, deviating from the essential feminist assumption that one always has to take personal experience as a starting point: in *The Second Sex* Beauvoir however avoids speaking of herself.

Michèle Le Dœuff dicusses this problem in her book *Hipparchia's Choice*.[29] She also relates her own difficulty of being at the same time a woman, a philosopher and a feminist, directly to the case of "Beauvoir-Sartre".[30] She holds that since classical antiquity women had gained access to philosophy by performing the role of the loving admirer and the devoted disciple. *The Second Sex*, which is based on existentialist ethics, could be seen as a sort of wedding gift to Sartre, in which Beauvoir gives a singular confirmation of the validity of Sartre's work: "Your thought makes possible an understanding of women's condition, your philosophy sets me on the road to my emancipation – your truth will make me free."[31] Alluding to the relation between Héloïse and Abelard Michèle Le Dœuff refers to this phenomenon as the "Héloïse complex".[32] Why, she wondered, had the brilliant student of philosophy later left philosophy to Sartre?

Toril Moi picked up this question in her book of 1994, agreeing with Michèle Le Dœuff when comparing Simone and Jean-Paul with Héloïse and Abelard. For Toril Moi Michèle Le Dœuff had explained very well why Beauvoir

---

[29] See: Michèle Le Dœuff, *Hipparchia's Choice. An Essay Concerning Women, Philosophy*, Oxford UK & Cambridge MA: Blackwell 1991, p. 47.
[30] Ibidem, p. 1 and p. 45.
[31] Ibidem, p. 59.
[32] Ibidem, p. 162, 163.

had surrendered as a philosopher in relation to Sartre. In her *Memoirs of a Dutiful Daughter* Beauvoir recounted that in 1929 on a summer morning at the Jardin du Luxembourg in Paris, after trying to demonstrate to Sartre her pluralistic morality in a three hour long debate, she arrived at the conclusion that her arguments could not stand up to his. Her philosophical defeat had led to the painful loss of her faith in her sovereign and exclusive status as a thinking being.[33] At the same time – so Toril Moi – this would enable Beauvoir to equip Sartre with all phallic qualities, because if she were unable to admire him, she would not be able to love him.[34] And so Beauvoir was to put herself intellectually and philosophically in second place after Sartre for the rest of her life. Furthermore, Beauvoir guarded the myth of unity between herself and Sartre as one of the most fundamental elements of her identity. However much she had tried to liberate herself from some negative aspects of this myth, it remained the only untouchable dogma of her life.[35] Toril Moi's interest focuses as a matter of priority on Beauvoir's person as the title of her book already suggests: *Simone de Beauvoir: The Making of an Intellectual Woman*. In her work she assumes that there can be no methodological difference between "life" and "text". Just like for Freud

---

[33] Toril Moi, *Simone de Beauvoir. The Making of an Intellectual Woman*, p. 19.

[34] Ibidem, p. 18. Toril Moi quotes a passage from Beauvoir's memoirs: "If in the absolute sense a man, who was a member of the privileged species and already had a flying start over me, did not count more than I did, I was forced to the conclusion that in relative sense he counted less: in order for me to recognize him as my equal, he would have to prove himself my superior."

[35] Ibidem, p. 30.

the person only reveals itself in a text Beauvoir reveals herself through an intertextual network of narrative, philosophical and autobiographical texts and letters.[36]

Does this apply in reverse as well? Can and should Beauvoir's work be interpreted in respect to her person? Should the interpretation of *The Second Sex* take into account that Beauvoir was a woman, that she was the longtime companion of a famous philosopher and a lot more besides? Toril Moi holds an ambivalent view thereon. On the one hand she mixes the personal and the philosophical regarding Sartre and Beauvoir, on the other hand she appears quite tired of the permanent discussion of who was superior to whom intellectually. Furthermore, she accuses the patriarchal criticism of presupposing that the work of an intellectual woman has to be judged in relation to that of her lover.[37] In turn she criticizes those feminists who judge Beauvoir all too strictly, even though it is no surprise that these women would feel the need to separate themselves from such a strong mother imago. For Moi the largest paradox is that feminists, who were influenced by the French feminist theory developed in the 1970s, either ignored Beauvoir or depreciated her as a theoretical fossil.[38]

By the end of the 1970s a stage of feminism had developed which Iris Young later on referred to as "gynocentric feminism".[39] Femininity was not regarded as the cause for discrimination of the woman but represented a positive value, from which the creation of a new and better world

---

[36] Ibidem, p. 3 and 4.
[37] Ibidem, p. 126.
[38] Ibidem, p. 182.
[39] Iris Marion Young, *Humanism, Gynocentrism and Feminist Politics*, in: *Women's Studies International Forum*, Vol. 8, Nr. 3, p. 173-183.

could be undertaken. According to Young, suppression does not consist in denying female self-realization, as postulated in humanist feminism, which was supported by Beauvoir and most feminists of the 19th and 20th century, but rather in rejecting and depreciating the female body and female activities through an all too instrumentalist and authoritative male culture. Contrary to humanist feminism that presupposes the ideal of an universal human nature demanding equal rights and equal chances for everybody and which therefore is also labeled as theory of equality, gynocentric feminism affirms uniqueness and difference and is therefore often referred to as difference feminism. Young accuses Beauvoir of equating being human with masculinity without questioning the common definitions of being human in Western society and of devaluating traditional female activities like motherhood and housework in the same way as patriarchal culture. Through the differentiation of transcendence and immanence, Beauvoir's ontology would reproduce the opposites of culture and nature, freedom and bare life, mind and body rooted in Western tradition.

The reproach of dualism is one of the most central criticisms directed towards *The Second Sex*. It can be traced back to the earliest receptions of Beauvoir's work, through all phases of feminist theory, right up until the present debate.[40] In *Gender Trouble,* Judith Butler writes: "Despite my own previous efforts to argue the contrary, it appears that Beauvoir maintains the mind/body dualism, even as she proposes a synthesis of those terms. The preservation of

---

[40] See Jo-Ann Pilardi, *Feminists Read The Second Sex*, in: Margaret A. Simons (ed.), *Feminist Interpretations of Simone de Beauvoir*, University Park: The Pennsylvania State University Press 1995, p. 29-45.

that very distinction can be read as symptomatic of the phallologocentrism that Beauvoir underestimates."[41] Most feminist authors agree that the differentiation between transcendence and immanence and the devaluation of the female body and traditional female activities interrelated with it is an expression of male-dominated thinking. Differences arise only when trying to ascertain from whom the concept of the mind/body dualism originated: Sartre or Beauvoir? Judith Butler's viewpoint is indicative of those feminists who believe that Beauvoir adopted Sartre's existentialism: "The radical ontological disjunction in Sartre between consciousness and the body is part of the Cartesian inheritance of his philosophy. Significantly, it is Descartes' distinction that Hegel implicitly interrogates at the outset of the 'Master-Slave' section of *The Phenomenology of Spirit*. Beauvoir's analysis of the masculine Subject and the feminine Other is clearly situated in Hegel's dialectic and in the Sartrian reformulation of that dialectic in the section on sadism and masochism in *Being and Nothingness*. Critical of the very possibility of a 'synthesis' of consciousness and the body, Sartre effectively returns to the Cartesian problem that Hegel sought to overcome. Beauvoir insists that the body can be the instrument and situation of freedom and that sex can be the occasion for a gender that is not a reification, but a modality of freedom."[42]

Michèle Le Dœuff, Judith Butler and Toril Moi see voluntarism as the source of evil in Sartre's existentialism, a philosophy, that – according to Toril Moi – had forced

---

[41] Judith Butler, *Gender Trouble: Feminism and the Subversion of Identity*, New York & London: Routledge, 1999, p. 17.
[42] Ibidem, p. 17, footnote 21.

Beauvoir to argue for free choices of the individual, despite being aware of the social conditioning of women's lives.[43] The description of female sexuality in Sartre's *Being and Nothingness* was criticized in particular for being sexist and created resentment. The existentialist project – according to Moi – is represented as movement upward or forward, since male erection and ejaculation underlie the notion of the project. "If Sartre describes the project metaphorically as a 'throwing forward' or a 'lifting up', for Beauvoir the non-project becomes a 'fall' or 'degradation'. To launch concrete projects in the world becomes a case of 'throwing oneself forward' into the future: on this logic only linear projects count. Repetitive, circular, cyclical, erratic or random modes of activity, ranging from flirtation to housework, can never hope to be classified as authentically transcendent."[44] It is striking that hardly anyone took the effort to prove these accusations in Sartre's texts, let alone entering into a serious discussion with his philosophy.

However, there are also other interpretations concerning the transcendence-immanence problem in Beauvoir's work. At the end of the 1990's research on Beauvoir turns towards her philosophical contributions, intending to elaborate her autonomy as a philosopher in her own right, independent from Sartre. So for example Sartre's existentialism is no longer seen as the sole influence on Beauvoir in *The Second Sex*: other influences are now examined. Eva Lundgren-Gothlin points out the importance of the influence that Kojève's Hegel interpretation had on *The Second Sex* and thereby opposes the prevalent opinion that Beau-

---

[43] Toril Moi, *Simone de Beauvoir*, p. 34. See also p. 60.
[44] Ibidem, p. 152.

voir was only able to access Hegel's dialectic through Sartre's own reformulation in *Being and Nothingness*.[45] In contrast to Sartre's ahistorical position, *The Second Sex* gains a historical aspect through Kojève's Hegel interpretation and also the possibility of overcoming the conflict through reciprocal recognition. According to Lundgren-Gothlin Beauvoir had succeeded in developing a social philosophy long before Sartre, seeking on the one hand the reasons for suppression, and offering on the other hand a means of liberation. However, in Hegel's theory as well as in Kojève's, women would be excluded from the fight for recognition. This distinction between the sexes is made explicit when Kojève says: "The family is a *human* by the fact that its (male) members struggle for recognition and have slaves; they are accordingly Masters."[46] Lundgren-Gothlin emphasizes that, in her opinion, Beauvoir does not equate the woman – as other interpretations of Beauvoir do – with the servant, but regarded the woman as the "absolute Other" due to the fact that she never participated in the master-servant-dialectic.[47] While the man rose above nature, crossed and transcended it during his fight for recognition, the woman remained closer to nature due to her female body and her ability to give life, thus making it possible to become a mediator for man, mediating between nature and man himself. Beauvoir would have demanded that women have to free themselves from nature just as men do: on the one hand, through the Marxist concept of the par-

---

[45] Eva Lundgren-Gothlin, *Sex & Existence. Simone de Beauvoir's 'The Second Sex'*, Hanover and London: Wesleyan University Press, 1996, p. 67.
[46] Ibidem, p. 72.
[47] Ibidem, p. 72.

ticipation in the work process, and on the other hand through the free disposal of their body through autonomous birth control.[48] Both Hegel and Marx associated motherhood more to animalistic activities than to human ones and, according to Lundgren-Gothlin, unfortunately instead of criticizing this androcentric point of view Beauvoir adopted it.[49] Like Hegel, Beauvoir contrasts life and spirit and saw the devaluation of the woman as a necessary step towards the development of mankind. The misogynic dualism in Beauvoir's work does not therefore stem from Sartre's existentialism – as has been assumed until now – but rather is due to the fact that Beauvoir connected Hegel's master-servant-dialectic to a theory of history inspired by Marx in order to show the suppression of the woman as a collective, social and historical phenomenon. In *Being and Nothingness* Sartre makes no specification of what should be counted as an intentional action. Thus, women's domestic labor could very well fall into the category of transcendence. In *The Second Sex*, however, through the influence of Hegel and Marx, transcendence attains a specific meaning due to the content it obtains from certain gender-specific activities within society. The area of society, where male activities traditionally take place is called transcendence, whereas immanence is equated with the area of traditional female activities.[50]

Many interpreters of Beauvoir agree that her independence from Sartre is also shown in the fact that she concerned herself with social questions long before Sartre.

---

[48] Ibidem, p. 80.
[49] Ibidem, p. 81.
[50] Ibidem, p. 242.

"Without this shift from Sartrean ontology to sociology and politics, *The Second Sex* could not have been written."[51] Sonia Kruks points out that Beauvoir had already anticipated many of the ideas, which Sartre later realized in *Notebooks for an Ethics* and *Critique of Dialectical Reason*. She emphasizes Beauvoir's essential influence on Sartre's entire intellectual work[52]: the absolute and the radically individualistic concept of freedom elaborated in *Being and Nothingness* is being replaced by a more nuanced and socially mediated concept of freedom.[53] She points out that Beauvoir had already demonstrated in 1945 in her review of Merleau-Ponty's *Phenomenology of Perception* in *Les Temps Modernes*[54] that contrary to Sartre, the subject in Merleau-Ponty's work is never a pure for-itself. Later on, in 1955, Beauvoir went back to her analysis of 1945, now claiming that Sartre's philosophy was after all, like Merleau-Ponty's, a philosophy of embodied subjectivity and intersubjectivity.[55] Nevertheless, Kruks insists that Beauvoir's concept of the subject, as an embodied consciousness and as a socially situated and conditioned freedom lies closer to Merleau-Ponty's work than to that of Sartre. She claims that Beauvoir's development of a new concept of

---

[51] Toril Moi, *Simone de Beauvoir. The Making of an Intellectual Woman*, p. 151.
[52] Sonia Kruks, *Teaching Sartre About Freedom*, in: Margaret A. Simons (ed.), *Feminist Interpretations of Simone de Beauvoir*, University Park Pennsylvania State University 1995, p. 94; see also: Sonia Kruks, *Retrieving Experience. Subjectivity and Recognition in Feminist Politics*, Ithaca and London: Cornell University Press 2001, p. 27-51.
[53] Ibidem, p. 81.
[54] Simone de Beauvoir, „La Phénoménologie de la Perception de M. Merleau-Ponty", in : Les Temps Modernes, 1.2 (Nov. 1945), p. 363-367.
[55] Sonia Kruks, *Teaching Sartre about Freedom*, p. 88.

subjectivity had begun already in 1944 in *Pyrrhus et Cinéas*.[56] The concept of the interdependence of free subjects was supplemented in 1947 in *The Ethics of Ambiguity* with the concept of socially embedded subjectivity, leading to a new concept of the subject in 1949 in *The Second Sex*, namely the subject as embodied.[57] Beauvoir shows strength in having developed a theory of oppression which showed the social conditioning of women, without rejecting the concept of individual freedom, however much women may have been oppressed, positioning her concept of subjectivity between the concept of the free and responsible individual on the one hand, and the post-structuralistic dissolving of the subject on the other.[58]

In *Philosophy as Passion: The Thinking of Simone de Beauvoir* Karen Vintges points out striking similarities between Sartre's existentialism and what has been called "postmodernism": both share the idea of the impossibility of universal moral theories – God and truth are dead – and thus the foundations of morality have disappeared.[59] Compared to the anarchism or "nomadism" of Sartre, Beauvoir emerges as a "moralist".[60] Time and again she had defended existentialism against accusations that it contained elements of nihilism, and tried to develop an existentialist

---

[56] Sonia Kruks, *Beauvoir: The Weight of Situation*, in: Elizabeth Fallaize (ed.), *Simone de Beauvoir. A Critical Reader*, London and New York: Routledge 1998, p. 45, see also p. 59.
[57] Ibidem, p. 44.
[58] Ibidem.
[59] Karen Vintges, *Philosophy as Passion. The Thinking of Simone de Beauvoir*, Bloomington and Indianapolis: Indiana University Press 1996, p. 5.
[60] Ibidem, p. 88.

ethics. Unlike Sartre, she had seen within existentialist philosophy a place for friendship, generosity and love.[61]

Debra Bergoffen, too, claims that Beauvoir had, parallel to an "ethics of the project" oriented on Hegel's struggle for recognition, developed an "ethics of the erotic", the erotic underlying as a phenomenological-existential and ethical category our primary orientation to the world and to others.[62] According to Bergoffen both ethics result from a revision of intentionality being split into two conflicting moments by Beauvoir: a moment that discloses being, and a moment that identifies the disclosing "I" with the being it discloses. For Bergoffen Beauvoir's account of the first intentional moment echoes Husserl and Merleau-Ponty, whereas the second echoes Hegel and Sartre.[63]

Both Bergoffen and Vintges see in Beauvoir's conception of emotion as a positive experience a break with Sartre's solipsism, allowing to make room for love, solidarity and friendship as a moral attitude. Unlike Bergoffen in her "ethics of the erotic", Vintges claims that in the course of her life at the latest in her novel *The Mandarins* Beauvoir had developed an "ethics as art of living" comparable to Michel Foucault's "ethics as care of the self".[64] But whereas Beauvoir tried to develop in *The Ethics of Ambiguity* a positive normative ethics in terms of Kant, she later rejected the Kantian type of ethics, which knows absolute moral laws. Nevertheless she adhered to the universal prin-

---

[61] Ibidem, p. 46 and p. 60.
[62] Debra Bergoffen, *The Philosophy of Simone de Beauvoir. Gendered Phenomenologies, Erotic Generosities*, Albany: State University of New York Press 1997.
[63] Ibidem, p.76, 77.
[64] Karen Vintges, *Philosophy as Passion*, p. 86.

ciple of freedom for all and the "moral exigence" of "willing oneself free".[65] Vintges defines Beauvoir's concept of an "ethics as art of living" as follows: "in the name of our freedom, we must create ourselves as an individual identity, styling and developing our daily behavior in all its aspects, with the aim of contributing concretely to the quality of the life of others."[66] In contrast to Foucault, who elevates life to a work of art and whom Vintges accuses of an "aestheticistic elitism"[67], the aesthetic moment in Beauvoir's work would represent only the form and not the content: "art of living for her is the art of life and not living as work of art"[68]. Following the existentialist demand for articulating the essence of both the human condition in general and its subjective and temporary nature in concrete, the philosophical novel represented for Beauvoir the adequate medium for an ethics as art of living, offering the middle ground between pure philosophy and pure literature.[69] Therewith, Beauvoir can be situated close to postmodernist philosophers who argue that philosophy and literature are interwoven.[70] In her further argumentation, Vintges increasingly places Beauvoir as a person into the foreground: Beauvoir's work, especially her autobiography, can be regarded as her attempt to create a coherent identity for herself.[71] In this however, Beauvoir aimed at a certain identity, namely that

---

[65] Ibidem, p. 69.
[66] Ibidem, p. 94.
[67] Ibidem, p. 162
[68] Ibidem, p. 162
[69] Ibidem, p. 76.
[70] Ibidem, p. 161.
[71] Ibidem, p. 89.

of an intellectual woman.[72] Her life project consisted of unifying two conflicting identities: being a woman, and being an intellectual.[73] It was essential for Beauvoir to be accepted as a woman. She wanted to belong to the "second sex" "not to a third".[74] That was also the reason why Beauvoir did not define herself as a lesbian: from her viewpoint, homosexuals constituted the third sex. Only her lifelong relationship to Sartre had guaranteed that she never lost her status as a woman in spite of being an intellectual.[75] Beauvoir had not dared to position her work as being philosophical because she thought a philosophical identity would detract from her identity as a woman. Beauvoir's philosophical analysis of the relative identity of women must be seen therefore in the light of her own experience with Sartre. According to Karen Vintges in *Philosophy as Passion*, it was not only Beauvoir's work but also her own life which had revolved around the problem of women's relative identity: the attempt to solve this problem had turned her philosophizing into a passion.[76]

Identity in general and the identity as a woman in particular seems to be something extremely unstable. Postmodernist feminists question a fixed, pregiven feminine identity: "If there is something right in Beauvoir's claim that one is not born, but rather *becomes* a woman", Judith Butler writes in *Gender Trouble*" it follows that *woman* itself is a term in process, a becoming, a constructing that

---

[72] Ibidem, p. 120.
[73] Ibidem, p. 164.
[74] Ibidem, p. 173.
[75] Ibidem, p. 175.
[76] Ibidem, p. 177.

cannot rightfully be said to originate or to end."[77] One could expand Beauvoir's theory radically, so that "woman" need not necessarily be the cultural construction of the female body and "man" need no longer interpret male bodies but rather new, expanded categories could emerge, that go beyond the binary man-woman and disrupt the heterosexual matrix.[78]

The feminist discussion of the last years has revolved around the problems connected with a possible postmodernist loss of the subject of feminism. What would feminism fight for if there were no longer any women, if there were no more unquestionable things women have in common? In *Retrieving Experience* Sonia Kruks points out that we should retrieve the rich heritage of existential thought considering women's embodied experiences in order to build affective bonds among women who are in many ways radically different from each other.[79] She proposes that there are certain stable notations, certain "invariants" to feminine embodiment, and that these may enable women to feel with the visible physical suffering of other women more easily than that of men. Referring to Beauvoir' existential philosophy one would find, that the embodied subject, although not the site of an untrammeled freedom, is more than the plaything of social and discursive forces, as postmodernists want us make believe. [80]

---

[77] Judith Butler, *Gender Trouble*, p. 43.
[78] Ibidem, p. 142.
[79] Sonia Kruks, *Retrieving Experience. Subjectivity and Recognition in Feminist Politics*, Ithaca, New York: Cornell University Press 2001, p. 6. See also my review of this book in: *L'Homme. Europäische Zeitschrift für Feministische Geschichtswissenschaft*, Wien: Böhlau 2004, p. 172-175.
[80] Ibidem, p. 164.

In light of this, it is no wonder that the female body again comes into the foreground of further investigations. In *What is a Woman* Toril Moi emphasizes the importance of Beauvoir's existential philosophy concerning the body.[81] According to Moi, by claiming that being a woman has to be seen as the background for all further discussions[82], Beauvoir had found a way of thinking about sexual difference which steers clear of the Scylla of having to eliminate her sexed subjectivity and the Charybdis of finding herself imprisoned in it. "To say that the sexed body is the inevitable background for all our acts, is at once to claim that it is always a *potential* source of meaning, and to *deny* that it always holds the key to the meaning of a woman's acts."[83] Beauvoir's feminist goal was to create a society enabling women to gain access to the universality as *women,* neither as imitations of men nor as sexless beings, which do not exist at all. Considering this, so Toril Moi, a new reading of Beauvoir would offer a way out of the "equality or difference" dilemma.

In her earlier book of 1994 on Beauvoir Toril Moi however had reproached the difference feminists of not understanding that Beauvoir's political plan differed radically from theirs. According to Moi, in taking for granted the assumption that effective feminist politics presupposes a theory of female identity, certain "critics fail to consider

---

[81] Toril Moi, *What is a Woman? And Other Essays*, New York: Oxford University Press 1999.
[82] Cf. Simone de Beauvoir, *The Second Sex,* p. xxi: "But if I wish to define myself, I must first of all say: 'I am a woman'; on this truth must be based all further discussions."
[83] Toril Moi, *What is a Woman? And Other Essays*, p. 201.

alternative positions".[84] For Beauvoir as for Sartre, "existence precedes essence" and therefore questions of identity become secondary to questions of action and choice. Toril Moi concluded then, that it is impossible to reach an understanding of Beauvoir's feminism without taking into consideration her vision of freedom.[85]

Although a lot has been said on Beauvoir's feminism of freedom, her philosophical concept of freedom has rarely been investigated and if so only certain aspects were explored in depth.[86]

---

[84] Toril Moi, *Simone de Beauvoir. The Making of an Intellectual Woman*, Cambridge MA: Blackwell 1994, p. 184.

[85] Ibidem, p. 184.

[86] Anderson, Thomas C., *Freedom as Supreme Value: The Ethics of Sartre and Simone de Beauvoir*, in: American Catholic Philosophical Association: Proceedings of the Annual Meeting, 50, 1976, p. 60-71; Arp, Kristana, *Conceptions of Freedom in Beauvoir's The Ethics of Ambiguity*, in: International Studies in Philosophy 31, no. 2, 1999, p. 25-34. de idem, *The Bonds of Freedom, Simone de Beauvoir's Existentialist Ethics*. Chicago and La Salle: Open Court 2001; John, Helen James, *The Promise of Freedom in the Thought of Simone de Beauvoir: How an Infant Smiles*, in: American Catholic Philosophical Association: Proceedings of the Annual Meeting, 50, 1976, p. 72-81; Kruks, Sonia, *Simone de Beauvoir: Teaching Sartre about Freedom*, in: Ronald Aronson and Adrian van den Hoven (ed), *Sartre Alive*, Detroit: Wayne State University Press 1991, p. 285-300; reprinted in: Margaret A. Simons (ed.), *Feminist Interpretations of Simone de Beauvoir*, University Park: Pennsylvania University Press 1995, p. 79-95; Kruks, Sonia, "Freedoms That Matter: Subjectivity and Situation in the Work of Beauvoir, Sartre, and Merleau-Ponty", in: de idem, *Retrieving Experience. Subjectivity and Recognition in Feminist Politics*. Ithaca and London: Cornell University Press 2001, p. 27-51; Moi, Toril, "A Feminism of Freedom: Simone de Beauvoir." In, *What is a Woman? And Other Essays,* New York: Oxford University Press

Part I
Ambiguity, Freedom, Morality

The conception of freedom[87] constitutes the basis for the entire philosophical work of Simone de Beauvoir. In her memoirs *The Prime of Life* she emphasizes: "liberty, the foundation stone of all human values, is the only end capable of justifying men's undertakings." [88] Rather than at once developing a complete theory of freedom she presents in her philosophical essay *Pyrrhus et Cinéas* those philosophical ideas which she had already discussed in her novel *The Blood of Others*. She reflects upon Sartre's *Being and Nothingness*, with which she was familiar from Sartre's manuscript and long joint conversations: Being exists in the form of projects, not determined by death – as claimed by Heidegger – but by certain goals. In *Pyrrhus et Cinéas,* besides discussing the sense of human projects in general, she touches another essential issue: that of the Other and the need to find some positive basis for morality.[89]

1999; Raynova, Yvanka B., *Liberty: The Destiny of Simone de Beauvoir*, in: Dharshana International, 105, January 1987, no. 1, p. 31-37
[87] The French *liberte* in Beauvoir's work has been translated in the literature with liberty or freedom. We use freedom in our text.
[88] Simone de Beauvoir, *The Prime of Life*, Harmondsworth: Penguin Books 1965, p. 549.
[89] Cf. Simone de Beauvoir, *The Prime of Life,* p. 549: "In the second section, my problem was to find some positive basis for morality."

In her philosophical essay *The Ethics of Ambiguity* Beauvoir attempts to extend the existentialist conception of freedom by differentiating between freedom and liberation. If freedom, as Sartre claims, is a characteristic of transcendence and thus of Being itself, if this freedom is a *donnée*, how can we properly regard it as an goal? The concrete possibilities offered to human beings are very often unequal. Beauvoir therefore does not regard freedom solely as the basis for an existentialist theory of morality, ontology, epistemology and social philosophy, but also as the final end for morality itself that has yet to be attained. In *The Second Sex* she demands the realization of a society that offers all men, women included, concrete possibilities to realize their projects. Freedom is now regarded in connection with the problem of the recognition of the subject and is placed into a broader social and political framework.

Beauvoir's concept of freedom was therefore subject to constant development and change. In the following this process of development will be explored hermeneutically and reconstructed critically in a detailed analysis.

Pyrrhus et Cinéas

In her first philosophical essay *Pyrrhus et Cinéas* Beauvoir approaches the problem of freedom from a specific perspective questioning the sense of human projects in general. In her memoirs *The Prime of Life* she points out that the dialog between Pyrrhus and Cinéas was very much like the one she had had with herself, noted in her private diary, on her twentieth birthday. When asked by Cinéas what he would do after having conquered Africa, Asia,

Arabia and India, Pyrrhus replies that he would then rest, whereupon Cinéas asks him why he would not prefer to rest immediately, without conquering anywhere. This "What use is it all?", she writes, had already spoken to her as an inner voice in 1927, long before the Second World War and long before Sartre's *Being and Nothingness* had "denounced the vanity of earthly pursuits in the name of the Absolute and Eternity."[90]

So *Pyrrhus et Cinéas* is permeated with an almost unbearable tension: the striving for an absolute goal, where the senselessness of having to transcend comes to a rest, at the same time demonstrating the impossibility of an absolute goal.[91] Gradually all possible absolute goals are traversed only to then be dismissed as un-realizable: the stoic silence is rejected as pure inwardness just as is the attempt to place God's will as the absolute goal; but also humanity as a whole can serve us neither in the form of solidarity, nor in the form of progress as the absolute goal. For within humanity one only comes in contact with certain people and one is always located in a certain situation.[92] However

---

[90] Simone de Beauvoir, *The Prime of Life*, p. 550.

[91] Hazel Barnes underlined in her debate with Margaret Simons that Beauvoir had just as many other people of her epoch searched for an Absolute, that could have been put in the place of the "lost God" and could have given her life a new direction and value. However, it should not be concluded from this that Beauvoir had anticipated Sartre's thoughts in *Being and Nothingness*, let alone developed them. Sartre emphasized the impossibility of justifying existence through a pre-assigned purpose by showing the effort of the human being wanting to turn himself into a thing that would be useful "for" something, like a hammer. Hazel Barnes, *Response to Margaret Simons*, in: *Philosophy Today*, Vol. 42, De Paul University Chicago, Illinois 1998, p. 29.

[92] Simone de Beauvoir, *Pyrrhus et Cinéas*, p. 60.

this concrete Other also poses a threat, because another person's project need not coincide with mine. Neither the battle against the Other, nor the devotion which consists in placing the Other as the absolute goal in order to devote oneself to him or her, represents a solution of the dilemma. As the only glimmer on the horizon of senselessness, Beauvoir lets the freedom of the Other flash up, for it would be the only reality that could not be transcended.[93]

But – and this will prove to be a large problem – certain demands are connected to the freedom of the Other: the other must be on the same level with me: only then can he/she justify my existence. "Our freedoms support themselves mutually like the stones of a vault, which is however not supported by any pillar. Humanity is entirely suspended in a void, which it creates itself by reflecting on its plenitude."[94] There is no other goal in this world but mine, no other place but the one I prepare for myself.[95] In the end no further criterion remains for an ethical judgment because: "which human being could judge the human being? On whose behalf does he want to speak?"[96] The life of a human being does not represent itself as advancement, but rather as a cycle that needs only to be affirmed: the question "why?" appears in this light only as an attack of bad mood or childlike exaltation.[97]

However, are all goals and plans of man now senseless? Let's take a closer look at Beauvoir's further argumentation.

---

[93] Ibidem, p. 100.
[94] Ibidem, p. 120.
[95] Ibidem.
[96] Ibidem, p. 123 – closing sentences of the essay.
[97] Ibidem, p. 122.

The Project

In her explanation of the concept of the project in *Pyrrhus et Cinéas*, Beauvoir is referring to Heidegger: "Man is *ahead of himself*, he is always *somewhere else*."[98] He is, true to his nature, not focused on himself, but on something else. Only in connection to something that is outside of himself he is himself. Man is endlessly more than what he *would* be, if he were reduced to what he is in this moment in time. "Every thought, every look, every striving is transcendence."[99] According to Beauvoir, we cannot do anything other than trespass everything that is given, for it is in our nature.[100] "Because the human being is a project, its happiness and joys can only be projects as well."[101] Thus Beauvoir regards every pleasure as a project, because every scent, every landscape that charms us, throws us out beyond ourselves. Thus Beauvoir seems to equate transcendence with the project itself. This however is not in accordance with her further argumentation, because if every thought and every glance were already both transcendence and project at the same time, it would be no longer necessary to posit oneself as transcendence through one's concrete projects: It would not then be possible to be cut off from one's own transcendence and to fall back into

---

[98] Cf.: "In its very structure, care is ahead of itself – Being already in a world – as Being alongside entities within-the-world; and in this structure the disclosedness of Dasein lies hidden." Martin Heidegger, *Being and Time*, Oxford UK & Cambridge USA: Blackwell 1995, p. 263.
[99] Simone de Beauvoir, *Pyrrhus et Cinéas*, p. 26.
[100] Ibidem, p. 27.
[101] Ibidem, p. 28.

immanence. Thus it would also be no problem if we turn towards absolute goals granting us security and peace, because even in this world of pre-assigned goals and values every glance and every thought would still be transcendence.

This is however not Beauvoir's intention. Throughout her essays *Pyrrhus et Cinéas* and *Ethics of Ambiguity* she proceeds in an unstructured and unclear manner and it proves difficult to deduce a coherent sense and draw conclusions from her texts. On the one hand Beauvoir emphasizes that in order to realize a project, no pre-assigned social or natural order must exist stipulating specific purposes and goals to man, for otherwise the person could not question the goal of its actions or choose freely: "he would not act at all".[102] On the other hand she points out that each activity of man is or at least should be seen as acting. Thus, Beauvoir dissolves the tension between the "Being-in-the-world", the being thrown into an already existing world with its pre-assigned purposes and goals, and the project as the potentiality-for-Being, for the benefit of the project.

But we shall find that Beauvoir in *Pyrrhus et Cinéas* does not always equate the human being with the project: "Emotionally drained humans, like the one described by Janet, are indifferent towards the most beautiful spectacles, because for them acting has ceased within them, because for them the flowers are not there anymore to be picked and smelled (…) for them no future, no trespassing, no pleasure exists."[103] Another possibility for Beauvoir to renounce acting is by dedicating oneself to another person, some-

---

[102] Ibidem, p. 46.
[103] Ibidem, p. 24.

thing that need not be painful as in the previous case cited, but that can even bring peace and happiness to the involved. If someone else needs me and if I position him/her as the absolute goal for me, being entirely dedicated to him/her and making his/her will my will, I give up the possibilities for my own projects: "Nothing is questionable anymore; I do not want to be more than a response to a call that challenges me."[104] One dedicates oneself, because one wants to do so, and one wants to do so because in this way one "hopes to attain one's Being."[105]

However, here we are confronted with something that Sartre calls the absurdity of freedom, namely that even the renouncing of freedom is a freedom: "In fact we are a freedom which chooses, but we do not choose to be free. We are condemned to freedom, (…), thrown into freedom or, as Heidegger says, 'abandoned'".[106] Beauvoir brings in *Pyrrhus et Cinéas* an example of the slave that likes to be enslaved, and that of the voluntary servant. "The servant that obeys decides to obey and this choice has to be renewed every moment."[107] If I want to find my happiness in dedicating myself to another person dictating to me his or her absolute goals, then I will abstain from my own project.

Thus the paradoxical situation arises, that when I am free to choose my goal, why should I not be free to choose this particular goal, namely to find my happiness in the devotion to others or to God. Beauvoir rejects this because it would mean to renounce my freedom, which consists of

---

[104] Ibidem, p. 70.
[105] Ibidem, p. 72.
[106] Jean-Paul Sartre, *Being and Nothingness*, New York: Philosophical Library, p. 484, 485.
[107] Simone de Beauvoir, *Pyrrhus et Cinéas*, p. 72.

never being restricted in my own free projects through pre-assigned goals.[108] Here it becomes evident why in *The Second Sex,* Beauvoir makes a distinction between happiness and freedom.[109] Happiness and freedom do not always have to be in accordance with each other, but rather contradict themselves quite often. This is for Beauvoir especially the case when society declares those condemned to stagnation as happy under the motto: "Is not the housekeeper happier than the working-woman?"[110] Beauvoir sees therein one of the reasons why the woman refrains from her independence: thus she can evade at once both an economic risk and the metaphysical risk of a freedom in which ends and aims must be achieved without assistance.[111] The concept of the project in Beauvoir's work stipulates therefore that the human being selects and sets his goals freely. Therefore no absolute goal should exist, because the nature of a freely chosen goal is such that it can be transgressed by being achieved. The senselessness of having-to-transgress is connected to the nature of freedom. My freedom is such that I do not subordinate myself to any given goals or purposes, but rather set my goals freely. The concept of the goal is so ambiguous for Beauvoir because the goal, although simultaneously a new starting point can and must nevertheless be striven for as a goal: "The freedom of the human being is based on this ability."[112] Beauvoir sees herein the paradox of being a human: although each goal can be transgressed, it can only be transgressed after having been first recog-

---

[108] Ibidem, p.72.
[109] Simone de Beauvoir, *The Second Sex,* p. XXXIV.
[110] Ibidem, p. XXXIV.
[111] Ibidem, p. XXVII.
[112] Simone de Beauvoir, *Pyrrhus et Cinéas,* p. 28.

nized as non-transgressable.[113] In this way, she agrees with Pyrrhus that he sets out to conquer.

But why did Pyrrhus set himself this very goal, why did he choose this very project? According to Beauvoir the single projects of a certain human being that often seem absurd to an outsider, must be seen in the context of the initial project of this person. "Every project has a temporal duration and comprises a multitude of single projects. One has to be able to differentiate between the projects that are in accordance with the main project, those that contradict it and those that are connected with it only by chance."[114]

Beauvoir only briefly broaches the complexity of the topic of the projects by referring to the importance of the initial project enabling us to understand the global meaning of the different choices of a human being and to understand their development and unity. Beauvoir circumvents this complex subject here by placing the project ultimately as "original and free."[115]

But what makes a project a project? Let us take this a step further and look at what Sartre has elaborated on this topic. The intention represents an essential element of the project. "We should observe first that an action is on principle *intentional*", emphasizes Sartre, "the careless smoker who has through negligence caused the explosion of a powder magazine has not *acted*."[116] Another central element is the human's ability of negating. It is possible to evaluate an encountered condition as negative and to set a

---

[113] Ibidem, p. 60.
[114] Ibidem, p. 75.
[115] Ibidem, p. 64.
[116] Jean-Paul Sartre, *Being and Nothingness*, p. 433.

non-existent condition as a desirable one, whereby negating is only enabled by freedom. Beauvoir quotes Sartre on this topic in *Pyrrhus et Cinéas:* "through the presence of the human being comes into the world what Sartre calls "négatités": emptiness, lack, absence."[117] Whereas Beauvoir maintains that some people refrain from making use of these possibilities, while others do not, so that one has to impose reforms on them with force,[118] Sartre proceeds more subtly. In *Being and Nothingness* he considers another aspect: it seems that sometimes we cannot speak about an active and conscious refrain from change. In so far as man is immersed in a certain historical situation, he does not even succeed in conceiving of failure and lacks within a certain political organization or a certain economy; "this is not, as is stupidly said, because he 'is accustomed to it', but because he apprehends it in its plenitude of being and because he cannot even imagine that he can exist in it otherwise."[119] Therefore, it is not the harshness of a situation or the sufferings that it imposes that makes us change the world. On the contrary, starting with the day when we can conceive of a different state of affairs a new light falls on our troubles and our sufferings and we decide that these are unbearable. This means that only by wrenching away from himself and the world that the worker can posit his suffering as unbearable and consequently can make it the motive for his revolutionary action. This implies that for consciousness there exists the permanent possibility of effecting a rupture with its own past, of wrenching itself

---

[117] Simone de Beauvoir, *Pyrrhus et Cinéas,* p. 94.
[118] Ibidem, p. 94.
[119] Jean-Paul Sartre, *Being and Nothingness*, p. 434.

away from it, so as to be able to consider it in the light of non-being: "Freedom is precisely the nothingness which *is made-to-be (is been)* at the heart of man and which forces human-reality *to make itself* instead of *to be.*" [120] For human reality being is equal with choosing himself. But that does not mean that I have the freedom to rise or to sit down, to enter or to leave, to escape or withstand danger, it does not mean that freedom is to be understood as a purely capricious, lawless, unfounded contingency.

Sartre gives a very descriptive example in *Being and Nothingness*: I start out on a hike with friends. After some hours, I can withstand my fatigue no longer and sit down. I am being criticized that I was free, and not forced by anybody to sit down and would be just as free to suppress my fatigue like the others until we reach the resting place. Admittedly, I could have acted differently, but at what price? The fatigue by itself could not have provoked my decision. Fatigue is only "the way in which I exist in my body. It is not at first the object of a positional consciousness, but it is the very facticity of my consciousness."[121] Objectively and in correlation to this non-thetic consciousness, the roads are revealed as interminable, the slopes as steeper, the sun as hotter, etc. But I do not yet *think* of my fatigue; I do not apprehend it as the quasi-object of my reflection. Nevertheless there comes a moment when I do seek to consider

---

[120] Ibidem, p. 440. Hazel Barnes translates Sartre's "est été" with "is made-to-be" instead of "is been". (See: Timothy O'Hagan and Jean-Pierre Boulé, *A Checklist of Errors in Hazel Barnes' English Translation of Jean-Paul Sartre, L'être et le néant*, British Society for Phenomenology, Norwich: UEA 1987, p. 23). I wish to thank Yvanka B. Raynova, translator of *L'être et le néant* into Bulgarian, for this information.
[121] Ibidem, p. 454.

my fatigue and to recover it. That is, a reflective consciousness is directed upon my fatigue in order to live it and to confer on it a value and a practical relation to myself. It is only on this plane that the fatigue will appear to me as bearable or intolerable. It will never be anything in itself but it is the reflective for-itself which, rising up, perceives the fatigue as intolerable. My companions are in good health – like me, as fit as me and they are for all intents and purposes "as fatigued as I am." How does it happen therefore that they endure their fatigue differently?[122] It proves that my companion perceives his tiredness as a devotion to nature, and therefore has more reason to endure it. This requires on the one hand a special relation of my comrade towards his body, and on the other hand towards everything that exists in the world outside of him. It presupposes a certain project concerning his body: the body makes woods and mountains exist for him, through himself and his body, he reveals their sense. My project however revolves around distrust of my body, a sort of "wishing not 'to have anything to do with it,' wanting not to take it into account."[123] Consequently, I would like to get rid of my tiredness. I myself am referred to my original project, namely to my being-in-the-world inasmuch as this being is a choice. Sartre compares this process of reverting further and further back to the initial project with Freud's Psychoanalysis.[124] But, as psychoanalysis interprets human reality alone through a regression from the present to the past, the dimension of the future does not exist for it; the human be-

---

[122] Ibidem, p. 455.
[123] Ibidem, p. 457.
[124] Ibidem, p. 458.

ing loses one of its ecstasies. According to Sartre, psychoanalysis should be applied in a reversed mode: "instead of understanding the considered phenomenon in terms of the past, we conceive of the comprehensive act as a turning back of the future toward the present".[125] Each action can only be understood as a project towards something that seems to be possible. To give in to tiredness, for instance, is equated to transcending the way that has to be mastered by giving it the sense of being too troublesome a way. Each special possibility is intertwined into a whole, and based on a "world background". Therefore, everything in the world can only be grasped in regard to a certain project of myself. Only in the totality of my projects is the steep mountain too steep for me, the troublesome way too troublesome for me. For someone else they would be just perfect for climbing or training. This leads us to the basic act of freedom as the choice of myself in the world; Sartre speaks of an initial project underlying all projects: the initial choice. This determines all other projects and is basic inasmuch as it determines my being. This initial project can be recognized in the way that it cannot be interpreted by way of another project, because this initial project is a totality.

According to Sartre, a special phenomenological method would be necessary in order to explain the initial project: existential psychoanalysis. This initial project that I am is a project that does not concern my relations to this or that special object of the world, but rather my Being-in-the-world as a totality. Yet the initial project is difficult to access. Beauvoir refers to this in connection with devotion. It is so complicated to want the best for someone else because

---

[125] Ibidem, p. 459.

one can never know the project of the Other, since as we have already seen, it is very hard to have clarity about one's own projects. "Not only is it not possible to know evidently and with certainty what is best (le bien) for the other; but neither is there *one* thing that is best, which is definitely the best option. One often has to make a choice between several 'bests', posed by different projects."[126] All I can do is to offer starting points for the other, to create possibilities he can utilize further.[127]

From the cases previously mentioned, two complex topics arise. One revolves around the project itself. How does it originate? Could it be that some people do not have projects at all, that they are not even aware of being capable of realizing their own projects? Is it possible to refrain from projects? Why do we set these specific goals and not others? How does the single project correspond with the initial project? Can I recognize the initial project or am I only fooling myself? Am I able to coordinate contradictory projects by any means?[128]

The other complex of problems deals with the realization of the projects. Do the goals and purposes within my project correspond with the goals stipulated by society? In order to be able to answer these questions an analysis of the existing situation is required. This is what Beauvoir attempts to do in *The Second Sex*. In *Pyrrhus et Cinéas* she already poses these questions that become relevant in *The Second Sex*. Her main interest is already visible here,

---

[126] Simone de Beauvoir, *Pyrrhus et Cinéas*, p. 77.

[127] Ibidem, p. 79.

[128] Beauvoir herself points out that the human projects are isolated and even contradict each other. "My being seems to be destined to remain forever broken into pieces." Simone de Beauvoir, *Pyrrhus et Cinéas*, p. 103.

namely the orientation towards the concrete. From an ontological perspective the human being is always transcendence and even a project, nevertheless, it is only through the realization of his/her projects that he/she posits himself/herself concretely as transcendence, otherwise he remains within the realm of immanence.

In *Pyrrhus et Cinéas* this subject is touched on at first only to be overshadowed by another problem, which also thematically runs through to *The Second Sex*, namely the need to justify one's existence. Beauvoir points out in *The Second Sex* that every individual that is concerned with justifying his existence perceives an endless need to transcend himself. For Beauvoir there is "no justification for one's present existence" other than its expansion into an endlessly open future.[129]

The Justification of Existence

It is striking that Beauvoir bases her explanation of the project almost exclusively on Heidegger and only refers to Sartre's *Being and Nothingness* in order to criticize Heidegger's approach that "the authentic project of man is Being for death".[130] The human being is present in the form of projects, which are however not projects geared towards death, but towards certain ends. Sartre had demonstrated that the human being is not a fixed being, as are objects and therefore the human being simply "is" not, but in every

---

[129] Simone de Beauvoir, *The Second Sex*, p. XXXV.
[130] Simone de Beauvoir, *Pyrrhus et Cinéas*, p. 61.

moment has to create himself through his self-projects.[131] All these occupations that the human being is engaged in, for example, hunting, fishing, writing books etc., are not distractions, nor an escape as seen by Heidegger, but rather moves towards Being: "man has to create himself, in order to be. He must transcend because he *is* not, but transcendence must be understood as plenitude too, because he wants to be: in the finite object that he founds, man finds a solidified reflection of his transcendence."[132] In order to illustrate the importance of objects based on human projects, Beauvoir reverts again to Heidegger: "As Heidegger says, there is no interiority for man, his subjectivity reveals itself only by his engagement in the objective world. There is no choice but the choice that has an effect on things: what man chooses, what he makes, what he projects, that is what he founds".[133] Man is trying to seize his Being continuously[134] in order to find a foundation and justification for himself. Beauvoir writes about her inconsolability in her youth due to not having considered herself as having a personality, but in contrast as having experienced others as in possession of a blinding originality. This was possible, she concluded, because emptiness can only be felt by everyone himself/herself, whereas the Other can be experienced from the outside as an object in the world, as something accomplished: "I, who is nothing, believe in his Being."[135] Perhaps this other can stop my search for Being because there remains the burning desire "to choose an end

---

[131] Ibidem, p. 64.
[132] Ibidem, p. 63.
[133] Ibidem, p. 62.
[134] Ibidem, p. 65.
[135] Ibidem, p. 68.

that cannot be transgressed, an end, that really is an end. A solid object could not stop me, but would it not be possible that another human being could do so?"[136] And in fact, in *Pyrrhus et Cinéas,* the Other is attributed with this central meaning. Every goal that I choose and set myself can be transgressed by me. If this were not the case, I would have set myself an absolute goal and taken away from myself the freedom to continue setting my goals freely. The Other, however, that realizes his freedom through placing his projects into an open future, possesses exactly the structure that I am looking for: by being always an open self-transgression, he/she can never be transgressed by me. He/she plays a central role: only the Other is able to justify my existence. Here a characteristic of Beauvoir's philosophy becomes apparent: the need for justification[137]: "we need others in order to find our existence and to make it necessary".[138] But it is not for 'others' that we write books or invent machines, nor do we write them for ourselves, because we do not exist before the project but instead we are made by the project. Transcendence precedes every goal, every justification, but from the moment we are thrown into the world, we want to escape its contingency and want to make our existence a necessary one.[139] In her later memoirs *All Said and Done* Beauvoir writes about the problem of the self: "Why am I myself?"[140] What gives my

---

[136] Ibidem, p. 69.

[137] Hazel Barnes emphasizes Beauvoir's desire to find an absolute justification of her existence. It is the desire to exist for someone else, or to be of use to someone. Hazel Barnes, in: *Philosophy Today*, p. 29.

[138] Simone de Beauvoir, *Pyrrhus et Cinéas*, p. 96.

[139] Ibidem.

[140] Simone de Beauvoir, *All Said and Done*, Harmondsworth Great Bri-

life its essential unity?"[141] Two factors, she writes, have provided this unity: the place that Sartre had always had in her life, and her faithfulness to her original project – that of knowing and writing: "Like all living individuals I sought to overtake my Being, to rejoin and merge with it. (...) I also wanted to realize myself in books that, like those I had loved, would be existing objects for others, but objects haunted by a presence – my presence"[142].

As soon as we are thrown into the world we want to escape the contingence of our life and look for a justification of our existence. As will be shown in the next chapter, *Freedom as a Process of Development: the Problem of Childhood* Beauvoir emphasizes that children need absolute values. Beauvoir writes about the sense of shock and scandal she experienced on noticing at the age of thirteen that there existed opinions aside from those of her father, for example, those of her best friend, who openly contradicted and criticized her father's opinion. In this back and forth of arguments between them "the absolute engulfed; I could not repose on anyone any more".[143] She had discovered that we have to deal with several freedoms, not just with *one*: "and because they are free, they do not accord."[144] Contrary to what Sartre claimed, as will be shown later on, the desire for the absolute and the tendency to flee from freedom is not so much based on the fear of freedom, but on the desire for a clear and sheltered world. This is how childhood is understood by Beauvoir, there are no

---

tain : Pinguin Books 1977, Paris : Gallimard 1972, p. 9.
[141] Ibidem.
[142] Ibidem, p. 38.
[143] Simone de Beauvoir, *Pyrrhus et Cinéas*, p. 101.
[144] Ibidem, p. 101.

contradictory claims and clear instructions are provided. Problems arise when different interests, different values, arise in the same community. It is precisely here that the dilemma of the Kantian ethics manifests itself for Beauvoir. This ethics makes it our duty to always act in such a way that the maxim of my actions can be the maxim of acting for all people; "but as we have seen", Beauvoir emphasizes, "the judgments of people cannot be reduced to a common denominator."[145] From this dilemma, we do not live in a world of harmony but of struggle. The problem is, that I cannot simply "be", I have to found and justify myself by realizing myself through my projects in the objects I create. This is the reason why I get into conflict with the projects of other people, because my projects can prove as obstacles for others or even contradict their projects. On the other hand there will be people that will help me to realize my projects. I also need the Other in order to carry my projects into the future. Inasmuch as there do not exist only helpful people, who are in accordance with my project and want to carry it into an endless future, I have to fight: "I fight to be."[146] Beauvoir stresses her conviction that: "My goal is to attain Being."[147] Being an artist she cannot be indifferent to the situation that surrounds her, "Thus I shall fight in order to make free people give the necessary place to my actions and my work."[148] But unfortunately the freedom of the others cannot be forced; I can only appeal to them. The respect for freedom – obviously a reference to Kant – is for Beau-

---

[145] Ibidem, p. 101.
[146] Ibidem, p. 111.
[147] Ibidem, p. 111.
[148] Ibidem, p. 112.

voir in this case not an abstract rule, but rather the basic requirement for the success of her efforts. Nonetheless she remains skeptical towards Kantian morality, as it leaves our own concrete being in the world unconsidered: "It is the error of Kantian morality to have rendered abstract our actual presence in the world; it uses only abstract formulas; the respect before humanity in general does not suffice to guide us, because we have to deal with separated and opposed individuals: the human person is both the victim and the executioner; must we let perish the victim, or kill the executioner? ".[149]

What, after all, are now the concrete criteria for human action? If I am only able to justify my existence by bringing it into being through realizing my projects in the form of concrete objects and if I need the Other not only for enabling and continuing my projects, but also for making possible the openness of the future , then I depend highly on the freedom of the Other. This however poses a large problem, for in real life not all humans are "free" and furthermore there are obstacles hindering us to approach those that are indeed "free". Therefore, first I have to fight against all who want to silence me, those that want to hinder me from expressing myself and making my appeal audible. Furthermore, the problem arises that above all people must exist "who are free *for me*".[150] In order for my appeal not to fade away into the void, humans that are ready to listen to me must always be close to me; these humans have to be on the same level with me. Therefore, I have to create situations for people to enable them to accompany and

---

[149] Ibidem, p. 91.
[150] Ibidem, p. 113.

transgress my transcendence. Beauvoir demands health, education, well-being and leisure for others "in order that their freedom is not consumed by fighting against illness, ignorance and misery."[151] The people have to be freed for freedom and this is unfortunately often not possible without force. Beauvoir compares the individual who liberates people for freedom with an expedition guide cleaving a new path and going back all the time to collect the latecomers and then rushing back to the front again to continue guiding the group. If some are not ready to follow him or even attempt to halt the march, he has to use force for his defense. The theories of Kant and Hegel on morality are, according to Beauvoir, only so optimistic because in denying individuality they also deny the possibility of failure. All force is failure, but we are condemned to failure: "It is through violence that one makes a man out of a child, a society out of a horde. To renounce fighting would mean to renounce transcendence, to renounce to be. But nevertheless no success will ever efface the absolute scandal of each single failure".[152]

In *Pyrrhus et Cinéas* Beauvoir tries to develop an "ethics of the project",[153] namely the ethical commitment for the realization of a world securing for all people in the same way the possibility of a free realization of their projects towards an open future. Thus a normative standard should exist on which all activities should have to be based: an activity should be classified to be good if its aim is to

---

[151] Ibidem, p. 115.
[152] Ibidem, p. 117.
[153] See also: Debra Bergoffen, *The Philosophy of Simone de Beauvoir*, p. 45-71.

achieve for itself and others this privileged position: to set freedom free. Nonetheless the essay ends in an almost Nietzschean manner.[154] Human life is not an advancing, but rather a cycle that has to be affirmed. All values attain their meaning in the world only by the individual projects, from which standpoints can be defined and goals can be fixed, from which notions like progress and utility can acquire their meaning. From these individual positions it is not possible to judge a human being, let alone to implement a valid standard for everyone. "Which man could judge man? In which name would he have to speak."[155]

In Beauvoir's philosophical essay *Pyrrhus et Cinéas* many questions remain unanswered and many contradictions arise. She certainly sees the problem that arises from an ethics of the project, in which the Other is the means to attain my ends. As a way out of the dilemma the concept of generosity emerges on the horizon, which comprises turning to the Other without any intent, without hoping for an advantage for the realization of one's own projects, but rather to meet someone for the sake of himself/herself without wanting him/her to do something for us. However this thought is not elaborated any further.

Beauvoir writes in her memoirs *The Prime of Life* that she wanted to address various problems with this essay that had come about after the occupation of France and that she had dealt with in her novel *The Blood of Others*. The hero of the novel had refused for a long time to act. The occupa-

---

[154] Hazel Barnes points out that Beauvoir, as well as Sartre were influenced by Nietzsche during their adolscence. Nietzsche had already indicated the absurdity of looking for the absolute in a contingent world where God is dead. In: *Philosophy Today*, p. 29.

[155] Simone de Beauvoir, *Pyrrhus et Cinéas*, p. 123.

tion of France by the Germans made him accept force after years of pacifism. Beauvoir is referring here to Kirkegaard: "A truly moral human being cannot have a clear conscience; it applies its freedom only with 'Fear and shiver'".[156] Thus the question of guilt plays an important role. In the end the hero of the novel is abdicated from his guilt at the deathbed of the woman whose death he was responsible for: "You are never any more than an instrument in another person's destiny", she told him. "No external factor could possibly encroach upon freedom of choice: I willed my own death."[157] From this, so comments Beauvoir in her memoirs, the hero had concluded that each individual has the right to follow his/her inclination, if it leads to a worthwhile goal. During the War, the world as Beauvoir saw it had turned into chaos and she searched for a new moral orientation, for new principles and goals. In her memoirs, she termed this her "moral period".[158] In *The Ethics of Ambiguity,* her subsequent philosophical essay that was published right after the Second World War, Beauvoir turns towards this problem of morality.

The Ethics of Ambiguity

The Ethics of Ambiguity is the one work of Beauvoir dealing explicitly with the concept of freedom. In *The Second Sex* Beauvoir rejects any ethics of happiness by pointing out that her perspective is that of an existentialist eth-

---

[156] Simone de Beauvoir, *The Prime of Life*, p. 542.
[157] Ibidem, p. 542.
[158] Ibidem, p. 547.

ics: "Every subject plays his part as such specifically through exploits or projects that serve as a mode of transcendence; he achieves liberty only through a continual reaching out toward other liberties. There is no justification for present existence other than its expansion into an indefinitely open future. Every time transcendence falls back into immanence, stagnation, there is a degradation of existence into the *'en-soi'*, the brutish life of subjection to given conditions – and of liberty into constraint and contingence. This downfall represents a moral fault if the subject consents to it; if it is inflicted upon him, it spells frustration and oppression. In both cases it is an absolute evil. Every individual concerned in justifying his existence feels that his existence involves an undefined need to transcend himself, to engage in freely chosen projects."[159]

The aim of this chapter is to lay out the central theses and principles of existentialist ethics that later on become the fundament of *The Second Sex*. The concepts of ambiguity and transcendence play a main role here, whereupon Beauvoir not only refers to Sartre, but also to other authors. Furthermore, it will be shown that in *The Ethics of Ambiguity* Beauvoir often neglects the existentialist approach in favor of the humanist and Kantian approach. Her main concern at this time was to defend existentialism against the accusation of anti-humanism. Thus, it is understandable that the commonalities with the humanist tradition are emphasized instead of the differences. Another reason is that Beauvoir was interested in an ethics of liberation, for which she needed a normative measure involving a "should". One has to take a decision – in order to be moral – for freedom

---

[159] Simone de Beauvoir, *The Second Sex*, p. XXXV.

and thus for morality: one has to will oneself free. "This means we have to effect the transition from nature to morality by establishing a genuine freedom on the original upsurge of our existence".[160] Beauvoir therefore builds upon the ontological freedom of Sartre, defining the human being in general as having an ethical dimension that does not only represent the starting point, but also the very end for the human being, in the form of an "absolute should". Therefore, when defining transcendence, a differentiation has to be made in Beauvoir's work between the phenomenological-existential dimension and the ethical dimension of freedom.

Beauvoir was motivated for this essay by the following intentions: firstly, the polemical intention to defend existentialism against the accusations from the Christian as well as from the Communist side and to dismiss their criticisms; secondly, the intention to clarify the misunderstandings that had arisen around Sartre's *Being and Nothingness*; thirdly, by the intention to create the particular morality that Sartre had announced at the end of *Being and Nothingness,* but had not fulfilled. As Beauvoir noted in her memoirs *Force of Circumstance*, she had mentioned while chatting with Misrahi that she thought it would be possible to base a morality on *Being and Nothingness*, "if one converted the vain desire to be into an assumption of existence",[161] whereupon Misrahi had suggested that she should write about this. After Camus had also asked her to write a study about action for an anthology, and after

---

[160] Simone de Beauvoir, *The Ethics of Ambiguity*, p. 25.
[161] Simone de Beauvoir, *Force of Circumstance*, p. 75.

Pyrrhus et Cinéas was received so well, Beauvoir felt encouraged to return to philosophy.

Freedom and Finitude

Death

It is not much of a surprise that Beauvoir opens her essay which she completed after the end of World War II with an issue that touched her particularly at that time: death. It is from this topic that she develops the problem of freedom. Never did her own death, or other people's, obse4ss her as violently as during those years, she writes in her memoirs *The Prime of Life*. Beauvoir had been dealing with death and the dizziness of nothingness which comes with it, since her adolescence. Through the Second World War, however, death became something with which she was confronted every day. "Misfortune became a daily possibility, and so did death. (...) few years more or less matter little when set against the freedom and peace of mind one achieves the moment one stops running away from death. There were phrases that I had always regarded as hollow and meaningless, the truth of which I now discovered in the most intimate fashion: you must accept death when there is no other means of preserving your life."[162] Beauvoir sets this very personal atmosphere right at the beginning of *The Ethics of Ambiguity* by quoting from one of Montaigne's essays: "The continuous work of our life is to build

---

[162] Simone de Beauvoir, *The Prime of Life*, p. 549.

death."[163] According to Beauvoir, all living creatures are subjected to this natural fact, a fact from which only man tries to escape. She accuses the philosophers in particular of trying to dissolve this ambivalence by negating death "either by integrating it with life or by promising to man immortality. Or, again they have denied life, considering it as a veil of illusion beneath which is hidden the truth of Nirvana."[164].

Death and the finiteness of the human being mark the starting point of Beauvoir's reflections within a personal context, as well as within the horizon of the philosophical and political tendencies of her time. The question of the sense of human efforts lies agonizingly above everything: the search for general well being often results in atrocities, many of Beauvoir's friends were killed during the War. Full of pain, she writes in her memoirs *The Prime of Life* about the death of her friend Bourla that his loss affected the entire world. And yet the world was full; no place was left for the one who lets his place go vacant. This separation was a kind of betrayal! (...) And one day she, too, would similarly be gone and forgotten. According to Beauvoir, death personifies loneliness, isolation and separation of men. It is not desirable; nevertheless one cannot desire to flee this curse. If our lives were infinite, they would merge into universal indifference. Though death challenges our existence, it also gives meaning to our lives. It may be the instrument of absolute separation, but it is also the key to all communication. [165]

---

[163] Simone de Beauvoir, *The Ethics of Ambiguity*, p. 7.
[164] Ibidem, p. 8.
[165] Simone de Beauvoir, *The Prime of Life*, p. 549.

In *The Ethics of Ambiguity,* Beauvoir develops those moral ideas that she had already brought up in her novel *All Men are Mortal* and which, as she mentions herself, had laid out the implications she had drawn from *Pyrrhus et Cinéas*. The focus lies now on comparing the project of the subjection of the entire universe with the temporality and the finite nature of existence. *All Men are Mortal* gave her the opportunity to elaborate in detail on the conflict between the standpoint of death, the absolute, and that of life, of the individual, and to continue developing her ideas on death that were inspired by the War. Fosca, the immortal hero of the novel, had attempted just like a Demiurge to rule the world for centuries from the outside until he learned through failing that humans are free and sovereign and cannot be possessed, but rather have to be served.[166] With this novel, Beauvoir writes in her memoirs *Force of Circumstance*, she wanted to express her criticism of Communism which following Hegel depicted mankind and its future as a monolithic individuality: she was attacking this illusion by embodying in Fosca this myth of unity.

Consequently Beauvoir turns in *The Ethics of Ambiguity* against all "those reasonable metaphysics, those consoling ethics with which they would like to entice us"[167]. Men are acutely aware of the paradox of their condition. They know themselves to be the supreme end to which all action should be subordinated, but the exigencies of action force them to treat one another as instruments or obstacles, as means. "Perhaps in no other age have they manifested their

---

[166] Simone de Beauvoir, *All Men are Mortal*, Cleveland: World Publishing 1955.
[167] Simone de Beauvoir, *The Ethics of Ambiguity*, p. 8.

grandeur more brilliantly, and in no other age has this grandeur been so horribly flouted. (...) There was Stalingrad and there was Buchenwald, and neither of the two wipes out the other."[168] Beauvoir turns decidedly against all those assuming, just as the Communists following Hegel, that the end justifies the means. "One can thus repose in a marvelous optimism where even the bloody wars simply express the fertile restlessness of the Spirit."[169]

Kant, too, does not escape from Beauvoir's criticism, because "for him genuine reality is the human person insofar as it transcends its empirical embodiment and chooses to be universal."[170] Whereas, for existentialists, Beauvoir emphasizes, it is not the impersonal universal human nature that is the source of values, but the plurality of concrete, particular men. From this arises the question: "How could men, originally separated, get together?"[171] This points to the real problem, which according to Beauvoir might prove to be unsolvable. Nevertheless she refuses to deny "*a priori* that separate existents can, at the same time, be bound to each other, that their individual freedoms can forge laws valid for all."[172]

As in *Pyrrhus et Cinéas,* Beauvoir carries on explaining in *The Ethics of Ambiguity* certain concepts that she had been already developing on a continual basis. She keeps to her own path without letting herself become too restricted from any other side, not even from Sartre, to whom she does not exclusively refer when defining the concept of

---

[168] Ibidem, p. 8.
[169] Ibidem, p. 8.
[170] Ibidem, p. 17.
[171] Ibidem, p. 1.
[172] Ibidem, p. 18.

ambiguity, as she had already done when defining the concept of the project in *Pyrrhus et Cinéas*.

The Concept of Ambiguity

Existentialism, according to Beauvoir, had "from the very beginning defined itself as a philosophy of ambiguity."[173] It was by affirming the irreducible character of ambiguity that Kierkegaard opposed himself to Hegel. In Beauvoir's own generation it was Sartre, she emphasizes, who in *Being and Nothingness* "fundamentally defined man, that being whose being is not to be, that subjectivity which realizes itself only as a presence in the world, that engaged freedom, that surging of the for-oneself which is immediately given for others."[174]

From the beginning of *The Ethics of Ambiguity* Beauvoir portrays the human being a "rational animal" that is attempting to "escape from his natural condition without, however, freeing himself from it. He is still a part of this world of which he is a consciousness. He asserts himself as a pure internality against which no external power can take hold, and he also experiences himself as a thing crushed by the dark weight of other things. At every moment he can grasp the non-temporal truth of his existence. But between the past which no longer is and the future which is not yet,

---

[173] Simone de Beauvoir, *The Ethics of Ambiguity*, p. 9.

[174] Ibidem, p. 10. In the English translation of *The Ethics of Ambiguity* by Bernard Frechtman (1948) Sartre's *en-soi*, *pour-soi*, is translated by *in-oneself*, *for-oneself*, while in the English translation of Sartre's *Being and Nothingness* Hazel Barnes uses *in-itself*, *for-itself*. I would prefer *for-itself*.

this moment when he exists is nothing. This privilege, which he alone possesses, of being a sovereign and unique subject admits a universe of objects, is what he shares with all his fellow-men. In turn an object for others, he is nothing more than an individual in the collective on which he depends."[175] As before in *Pyrrhus et Cinéas,* Beauvoir is referring in *The Ethics of Ambiguity* to different approaches without differentiating them any further. She does not only refer to Sartre, she does not see herself simply as his "interpreter" but is rather attempting to provide answers in a versatile, but sometimes unstructured manner to one of her central questions, namely: How do we cope with the desire for the absolute?

While asking this question, her description of ambiguity fluctuates between various approaches. In the aforementioned passage she refers not only to Sartre's existentialism, but also to Hegel. Beauvoir points out that in Hegel's work the individual is only an abstract moment in the history of the absolute spirit. She rejects Hegel's assumption in the *Philosophy of Right* that "the right of individuals to their particularity is equally contained in ethical substantiality, since particularity is the extreme, phenomenal modality in which moral reality exists".[176] For him particularity appears only as a moment of the totality in which it must surpass itself. According to Beauvoir, Hegel's notion of the individual as an abstract moment in the history of the absolute spirit can be explained by the first intuition of the system which, identifying the real and the rational, empties the

---

[175] Simone de Beauvoir, *The Ethics of Ambiguity*, p. 7.
[176] Ibidem, p. 17. See also G.W.F., Hegel *Philosophy of Right*, §154, University of Chicago 1952.

human world of its sensible thickness. Thus the uniqueness of the individual is denied and it can no longer reappear except on the natural and contingent plane. What remains is the absolute spirit as a subject. But: "who is this subject?", Beauvoir continues to ask.[177] Hegel had tried to reject none of the aspects of man's condition and to reconcile them all, but for the price of the surpassing of the individuals in the totality in which they get lost. As soon as one considers a system only theoretically and abstractly, one puts oneself, in effect, on the plane of the universal, the infinite. "That is why reading the Hegelian system is so comforting. I remember having experienced a great feeling of calm on reading Hegel in the impersonal framework of the Bibliothèque Nationale in August 1940."[178]

Contrary to Hegel, as Beauvoir states, Sartre's existentialism is confronted with the accusation of being "a philosophy of the absurd and of despair", which encloses man in a sterile anguish, in an empty subjectivity; "it is incapable of furnishing him with any principle for making choices. Let him do as he pleases. In any case, the game is lost."[179] Beauvoir points out, that on the one hand, previous ethics also had to emphasize the element of failure involved in the condition of man, because "for a being who, from the very start, would be an exact co-incidence with himself, in a perfect plenitude, the notion of having-to-be has no

---

[177] Ibidem, p. 105.
[178] Ibidem, p. 158. Hegel's *Phänomenologie des Geistes* (*Phenomenology of Spirit*), originally published in German in 1807, was translated into French in 1939 and Hegel's *Grundlinien der Philosophie des Rechts* (*Philosophy of Right*) in 1940.
[179] Ibidem, p. 10.

meaning."[180] On the other hand, she attempts to demonstrate that the failure described in *Being and Nothingness* is definite, but also ambiguous. She tries hard to outline a moral "should" for existentialism which explains the problematic conclusion of her essay.[181] At the same time she designs her own concept: rather than being a Hegelian act of surpassing, in existentialism we can speak about a conversion. "However, rather than being a Hegelian act of surpassing, it is a matter of a conversion. For in Hegel the surpassed terms are preserved only as abstract moments, whereas we consider that existence still remains a negativity in the positive affirmation of itself. And it does not appear, in its turn, as the term of a further synthesis. The failure is not surpassed, but assumed."[182]

Right at the beginning of the chapter entitled "Ambiguity", Beauvoir defines existence itself as ambiguous in the way "that its meaning is never fixed, that it must be constantly won."[183] This, however, must not be understood in the way that existence is "absurd", which would subsequently result in the impossibility of an ethics at all. One has to consider that "also the finished rationalization of the real would leave no room for ethics; it is because man's

---

[180] Ibidem, p. 10.

[181] Beauvoir concludes her essay with the statement that – "If it came to be that each man did what he must, existence would be saved in each one without there being any need of dreaming of a paradise where all would be reconciled in death." This ending is particularly striking as Beauvoir repeatedly points out that the ambiguity of the human being does not allow a final reconciliation, that our life will always be overshadowed by conflicts. Furthermore, she does not generate any criteria for this "should". *The Ethics of Ambiguity*, p. 159.

[182] Ibidem, p. 13.

[183] Ibidem, p. 129.

condition is ambiguous that he seeks, through failure and outrageousness to save his existence. Thus, to say that action has to be lived in its truth, that is, in the consciousness of the antinomies which it involves, does not mean that one has to renounce it."[184]

Ambiguity in Beauvoir's work could be understood as the following:

1. As non-identity resulting from the ontological basis of man as developed by Sartre saying that man is not what he is, but what he is not, man is at the same time transcendence and facticity.

2. As possibility to escape one's freedom. Man is able to negate his freedom "by losing himself in the object", subordinating himself to absolute values in order to thus realize himself "as a *being* who is escaping from the stress of existence."[185] Beauvoir sees in large parts of Sartre's *Being and Nothingness* a description of the serious man, getting rid of his freedom by claiming to subordinate it to values which would be unconditioned.[186] Escaping freedom is bad faith (mauvaise foi) consisting of only recognizing one part of existence- be it facticity or transcendence.

3. As non-coincidence: man cannot be considered "as being an essentially positive will",[187] thus he can never be in coincidence with himself, since being defined as negativity he is always at a distance from himself: "he can coincide with himself only by agreeing never to rejoin himself."[188] Beauvoir points out that inside man there is a per-

---

[184] Ibidem, p. 129.
[185] Ibidem, p. 46.
[186] Ibidem, p. 46.
[187] Ibidem, p. 33.
[188] Ibidem, p. 33.

petual playing with the negative, and he thereby escapes himself, his freedom.[189] We thus cannot speak of a steady character as Kant does; as the choice of his character which the subject makes is achieved in the intelligible world by a pure rational will, one cannot understand how the latter expressly rejects the law which it gives to itself. If man is defined as a pure positivity, no other possibility can be conceded to him, but the coincidence with himself.[190] Only existentialism takes evil[191] into account, just as religion does. Perhaps, so Beauvoir, this is the reason for judging existentialism so negatively[192].

---

[189] Ibidem, p. 33.

[190] Ibidem, p. 33.

[191] In her philosophical essay *The Ethics of Ambiguity* Beauvoir does not give us criteria that would allow the assessment of good and evil even though her efforts center around that topic over and over again. To answer the question: "Which action is good? Which is bad?" (p. 134), she proposes a method analogous to scientific or aesthetic methods: "of confronting the values realized, with the values aimed at, and the meaning of the act with its content." (p. 152). The word "evil" is used by Beauvoir in the following context: "There are cases where a man positively wants evil, that is, the enslavement of other men, and he must then be fought." (p. 136). Just as an objective is not supposed to be separated from the means, the means cannot be judged without the objective that is endowing its meaning, emphasizes Beauvoir. The lynching of a black person "is an absolute evil; it represents the survival of an obsolete civilization; it is a fault without justification or excuse" (p. 146)..Suppressing a hundred opponents is surely an outrage, but it may have meaning and a reason: "it is a matter of maintaining a regime which brings to an immense mass of men a bettering of their lot." (p. 146. Here freedom seems to be the criterion for good and evil. If the purpose of an act is the propagation or preservation of freedom then this act is a good one. Here the question arises whether the concept of freedom is not used as a new instrument for exercising and legitimizing power relations.

[192] Simone de Beauvoir, *The Ethics of Ambiguity*, p. 34.

4. As failure of man that consists "in his vain attempt to *be* God",[193] that means to posit himself as absolute ground for himself, failure therefore, is irrefutably a part of mankind as it is through this that man makes himself exist *as* man.[194] The disclosure of failure thus is the condition *sine qua non* of authenticity.

5. As temporality of man, which means that man *is* not only, but "makes himself", realizes himself only through his actions and through his lived life.

6. As irreducibility of human existence: man has to assume his finiteness: "not by treating his existence as transitory or relative but by reflecting the infinite within it, that is, by treating it as an absolute".[195] Man has a body made out of flesh and blood, he has feelings and passions and is always in a specific situation. He must not be regarded solely "as a human person, as Kant does, insofar as he transcends his empirical embodiment and chooses to be universal."[196] Neither must men be preserved only as abstract moments in the "fertile restlessness of the Spirit", as Hegel asserts.[197] Instead, for existentialism it is not the impersonal universal human nature that is the source of values, but the plurality of concrete, particular men projecting themselves towards their ends on the basis of situations whose particularity is as radical and as irreducible as subjectivity itself.[198] Since man is originally a negativity, no social upheaval, no moral conversion can eliminate this

---

[193] Ibidem, p. 12.
[194] Ibidem, p. 13.
[195] Ibidem, p. 130.
[196] Ibidem, p. 17.
[197] Ibidem, p. 8.
[198] Ibidem, p. 17.

lack which is inside his heart: "it is by making himself a lack of being that man exists, and positive existence is this lack assumed, but not eliminated."[199] However, no abstract wisdom can be based on an existence that turns away from being and only focuses on the harmony of being, for such a negation would vanish in the absolute silence of the in-itself. Thus, a reconciliation of the individual transcendences becomes unthinkable: they do not possess the passive indifference of a sheer abstraction, they are concrete and they dispute concretely being themselves. "The fundamental ambiguity of the human condition will always open up to men the opposing choices; (...) the plane of hell, the struggle, will never be eliminated; freedom will never be given, it will always have to be won."[200]

These different aspects make it clear that ambiguity in Beauvoir's work unifies various dimensions: an ontological, epistemological, ethical, as well as a social dimension, the latter becoming important in *The Second Sex*.

The text to follow aims to clarify these points by referring to the phenomenological tradition, in particular in reference to Sartre. Based on the assumption that Beauvoir's approach stands in special relation to Sartre's existentialism, even though she refers to other authors as well, Sartre's theory will be discussed in more detail. This is done with the intention of showing where Beauvoir stands in accordance with Sartre and where she differs from him to a large extent.

---

[199] Ibidem, p. 118.
[200] Ibidem, p. 118.

Freedom and Transcendence

The Ontological Dimension of Freedom

Beauvoir presupposes in all of her considerations the phenomenological-existentialist tradition, she builds upon it and develops it further in her own style. Beauvoir takes Sartre's results and questions at the end of *Being and Nothingness* as the starting point for her new morality which she tries to develop in *The Ethics of Ambiguity*. Therefore it seems necessary to point out at least some aspects of Sartre's ontology after briefly discussing the development of the phenomenological method.

Husserl's development of the phenomenological method by combining Bretano's concept of intentionality with his own method of the *Epoché* had been a turning point in the history of philosophy.[201] Mental processes such as perception or cognition can only be sufficiently understood if what they are aimed at is not taken as external and given, but as an integral moment of the processes themselves. But whereas Husserl understands the term transcendence in an essentialist way, because from his ontological viewpoint transcendence forms the essence of the human being, Sartre rejects essentialism and reinterprets thinking, cogito and thus transcendence as existence according to Heidegger. This way, the insistence, the being-in-the-world of man, is additionally emphasized. Husserl had still held the view that concrete existence was irrelevant in the elucidation of existence and thus had to remain unaddressed. Heidegger,

---

[201] See: Herbert Spiegelberg, *The Phenomenological Movement*, The Hague, Boston, London: Martinus Nijhoff Publishers 1982, p. 97.

however, considered putting existence, *Dasein*, in parentheses to be a mistake and went on to base the essence of man on *Dasein*, on his day-to-day care: the essence of *Dasein* lies in its existence.[202]

Sartre departs on a kind of Heideggerian analysis of Dasein from the for-itself as nothingness, in order to return in a regressive analysis to the origin of the negative that underlies the phenomenon of questioning and that we encounter in various ways. For any mode of questioning involves the possibility of negation. In this structure of consciousness lies the basis of human freedom: "Human reality is free to the exact extent that it has to be its own nothingness".[203] It is transcendence, that is to say, it is not something which initially *is* and then has to correlate with one or another pre-assigned purpose, but rather oppositely, it is "a being which is originally a project – i.e., which is defined by its end".[204] Therefore we can never speak of the essence, of the nature of man, because for Sartre essence is what already has been; as Hegel said "was gewesen ist"[205]. Existence, however, does not only encompass the past, but also the future, the undertakings and projects with their not-yet realized possibilities. By being located between the past, which is no longer, and the future, which is not yet, the ontological structure of man as freedom, transcendence, and existence is nothingness, which specifies him as a being that can realize a negating rupture with the world and himself. Man, therefore, is always something other than

---

[202] Martin Heidegger, *Being and Time*, p. 10.
[203] Jean-Paul Sartre, *Being and Nothingness*, p. 453.
[204] Ibidem, p. 453.
[205] Ibidem, p. 439.

what one can say of him. He is undeterminable. The for-itself escapes its existence as essence, it negates every fixed identity: it is that which it is not, by not being what it is, what means that existence as "ex-sistere," as a project, precedes essence as fixed determination.

This negating act through which, what appears as unchangeably "natural", can be negated towards a new possibility, towards something that does not yet exist, represents an "ontological characteristic"[206] of the human being; that being "through whom nothingness comes to the world"[207] and for which in "its Being, the Nothingness of its Being is in question."[208] This, however, does not mean that it would even provisionally be possible to annihilate the "mass of being"[209] which it posits before itself. That which can be modified is man's "relation"[210] with Being. Whereas Sartre, when discussing the being of things assumes the principle of identity[211] A=A (he speaks about the fullness of the in-itself), the for-itself as the ontological foundation of consciousness escapes identity inasmuch as it is "presence to self" implying the detachment of the self from itself. Thus, an impalpable fissure slips into being[212], the negative, the annihilating power, the nothingness as it is referred to by Sartre, which "is not", but is "made-to-be".[213] This noth-

---

[206] Ibidem, p. 23.
[207] Ibidem, p. 24.
[208] Ibidem, p. 23.
[209] Ibidem, p. 24.
[210] Ibidem, p. 24.
[211] Ibidem, p. 74.
[212] Ibidem, p. 77.
[213] Ibidem, p. 78.

ingness is always an "elsewhere"[214], it is the necessity for the for-itself always to exist in the form of "elsewhere", and thus only in relation to itself, for it carries intentionality as the basic structure in itself.

Human existence contains the annihilating power that enables man to suspend existing reality and to transcend it toward new possibilities. This becomes immediately tangible in fear. Nothing can guarantee what one is going to do next: The vertigo on the mountain demonstrates that I could jump down into the ravine, however, nothing guarantees that I will not do it. This is only possible because I am not determined. The "ego" does not have a privileged position, it is not an absolute that has created the universe, but on the contrary it is transcendence, coexisting with and obtaining all its substance from the world. Already in *The Transcendence of the Ego*, one of Sartre's earliest works, he points out that the spontaneity of consciousness cannot originate from the ego, but that on the contrary the transcending consciousness is an impersonal spontaneity, an incessant creation. According to Sartre consciousness is not the result of an act of recognition, it is in no way relative to experience because it is experience.

Sartre emphasizes that the for-itself shall not be regarded as an attribute of a "substantial" in-itself.[215] That was Descartes' illusion: the Cartesian substance preserves "the character of being-in-itself in its integrity, although the for-

---

[214] Ibidem, p. 78.

[215] Judith Butler criticizes Sartre in that his radical ontological disjunction "between consciousness and the body is part of the Cartesian inheritance of his philosophy." Judith Butler, *Gender Trouble*, p. 196, footnote 21 to page 17. Butler is representative for many feminist reproaches against Sartre without elaborating and justifying them.

itself is its attribute"[216]. For Sartre, on the other hand, the appearance of the for-itself as an absolute event refers to the effort of an in-itself to found itself; it corresponds to an attempt on the part of being to remove contingency from its being. This attempt however results in the annihilation of the in-itself, "because the in-itself cannot found itself without introducing the *self* or a reflective, annihilating reference into the absolute identity of its being and consequently degenerating into *for-itself*."[217] Therefore, the in-itself is not a substance of which the for-itself would be the attribute and which would produce thought without exhausting itself in that very production.[218] The in-itself simply resides in the for-itself as "a memory of being, as its unjustifiable *presence in the world*."[219] As a consequence the for-itself has only "a factual necessity; that is, it is the foundation of its *consciousness-of-being* or *existence*, but on no account can it found its presence."[220] The for-itself can only found and justify itself through its project, through its existence.

The upsurge of the for-itself as the annihilation of the in-itself and the decompression of being gives rise to the possible "as a way of being what one is – a distance from the self."[221] At the same time, however, the possible is "the *something* which the for-itself lacks *in order to* be itself.[222] The lack of being in human existence becomes manifest in

---

[216] Jean-Paul Sartre, *Being and Nothingness*, p. 84.
[217] Ibidem, p.84.
[218] Ibidem, p. 84.
[219] Ibidem, p. 84.
[220] Ibidem, p. 84.
[221] Ibidem, p. 96.
[222] Ibidem, p. 102.

value and desire. Men are determined by what they perceive as desirable.[223] In the human world the incomplete being, offering itself to intuition as a lacking one, is constituted in its being through the lacking, that means through what it is not: "it is the full moon which confers on the crescent moon its being as crescent; what- is- not determines what-is"[224]. Sartre defines the lack of for-itself, namely what is lacking, as "the self – or itself as in-itself"[225].

The ontological structure of freedom in Sartre's work has the consequence that we can never coincidence with ourselves, that we can never be identical with ourselves in the sense of the identity of concrete things in the world. We attempt to escape this nothingness that manifests itself to us in fear, this uncertain and unpredictable possibility through which we will not be in the following moment that what we had always believed to be. By fleeing into inauthenticity we negate this freedom, this being-for-itself and only regard ourselves as pure facticity, as pure immanence. However, it also means a kind of inauthenticity to flee into transcendence by denying that we are facticity too. The only possibility to achieve accordance with "oneself" again would be to create a synthesis from in-itself-for-itself.

Human reality wants to surpass "itself toward the particular being which it would be if it were what it is."[226] Already Descartes' second proof of God had shown the fol

---

[223] See: Yvanka Raynova: *La phénoménologie des valeurs et le problème du sacrifice chez Sartre*. In : *Bulletin de la Société Américaine de Philosophie et de Langue Française,* vol. V, Nr. 23, case 1993, p. 66-79.
[224] Jean-Paul Sartre, *Being and Nothingness*, p. 87.
[225] Ibidem, p. 89.
[226] Ibidem, p. 89.

lowing: the imperfect being surpasses itself toward the perfect being. In other words: "The being which is the foundation only of its nothingness surpasses itself toward the being which is the foundation of its being. But the being toward which human reality surpasses itself is not a transcendent god; it is at the heart of human reality; it is only human reality itself as totality." [227] Thus the for- itself is by nature only an "unhappy consciousness"[228] with no possibility of surpassing its unhappy state: "The being of human reality is suffering because it rises in being as perpetually haunted by a totality[229] which it is without being able to be it, precisely because it could not attain the in-itself without losing itself as for-itself." [230] Let no one reproach us for capriciously inventing a being of this kind, emphasizes Sartre: "When by further movement of thought the being and absolute absence of this totality are hypothesized as transcendence beyond the world, it takes on the name of God. Is not God a being who is what he is – in that he is all positivity and the foundation of the world – and at the same time a being who is not what he is and who is what he is not- in that he is self-consciousness and the necessary foundation of himself?"[231] The idea of man wanting to be God is according to Sartre a useless passion[232] and generally doomed to failure because all these projects tend "to sacrifice man in order that the *causa sui*[233] may arise."[234]

---

[227] Ibidem, p. 89.
[228] Ibidem, p. 90.
[229] Ibidem, p. 90.
[230] Ibidem, p. 90.
[231] Ibidem, p. 90.
[232] Ibidem, p. 615.
[233] The "ens causa sui" is according to Sartre what religions refer to as

Thus the passion of the human being is the passion of Christ "for man loses himself as man in order that God may be born."[235]

As long as the projects of human beings are part of the *spirit of consciousness*, that means as long as the totality of their choices of possibilities are determined by "the value of the ideal presence of the *ens causa sui*"[236] all actions are equivalent and doomed to fail as they all aim at sacrificing man in order that God may arise.[237] "Thus it amounts to the same thing" – emphasizes Sartre – whether one gets drunk alone or is a leader of nations. If one of these activities precedes over the other, this will not be because of its real goal but because of the degree of consciousness which it possesses of its ideal goal; and in this case it will be the quietism of the solitary drunkard which will take precedence over the vain agitation of the leader of nations."[238] The spirit of seriousness has according to Sartre two characteristics: it considers values as transcendent givens independent of human subjectivity, and it transfers the quality of "desirable" to their simple material constitution. For example, *bread* is "desirable because it is necessary to live (a value written in an intelligible heaven) and because bread *is* nourishing."[239] The spirit of seriousness posits the things in

---

God, ibidem, p.615.
[234] Ibidem, p.627.
[235] Ibidem, p. 615; See also: Yvanka B. Raynova: *L'etre et le néant, une lecture post-personnaliste*. In: *Études Sartriennes,* no.6, 1995, p.79-90.
[236] Ibidem, p. 627.
[237] Ibidem, p. 627.
[238] Ibidem, p. 627.
[239] Ibidem, p. 626.

themselves as a "desirable irreducible".[240] Thus it comes down to an objectification and substantification of values. Objects are mute demands, and man is nothing in himself but the passive obedience to these demands.[241]

Sartre concludes that ontology cannot formulate moral rules, nevertheless he ends *Being and Nothingness* with "moral perspectives" and the hope for having brought into consciousness to man his blind search for being and having pointed out that man "pursues being blindly by hiding from himself the free project which is this pursuit."[242]

Let's sum up the previous analysis.

Sartre defines "human reality", being, as a relation, as a project. Intentionality as the fundamental structure of human consciousness is always directed towards and tied to an "elsewhere". The human being is nothing but its projects, it is nothing else but the totality of its actions, nothing but its life. These acts however are not restricted generally to conscious, voluntary actions, nor are there certain actions that would be privileged in comparison to others, as shown by the example of the drunkard and the general. The freedom of the human being is not based on the freedom of the will as is the case in the tradition of philosophy but on transcendence, on the project. I am not free because I want to be free, but because of my ontological structure as freedom and transcendence. However, this freedom is absurd for I have not chosen to come to this world, nor to find myself at this place, in this environment and in this body and as such I am not free not to choose myself: I am con-

---

[240] Ibidem, p. 626.
[241] Ibidem, p. 626.
[242] Ibidem, p. 626.

demned to freedom. Once thrown into the world, there remains no other possibility than to permanently realize oneself in projects and all actions are considered as equal whether they are successful or not, whether it has to do with housework or raising children or politics or waging wars, even the lonely drunkard under the bridge pursues a certain project. Sartre is aiming at a process of awareness. At the end of *Being and Nothingness* he points out that the human being has to become aware of the fact that he has always been freedom, transcendence and project even if he is not aware of it or if he was deprived of it.[243]

Let's go back to Beauvoir now. Beauvoir is attempting to construct in *The Ethics of Ambiguity* an ethics based on Sartre's phenomenological ontology.[244] However, she does not only adopt his ontology, but modifies it. In contrast to Sartre she assumes that it is indeed possible to fall back into "bare facticity"[245], to live as pure in-itself.[246] This happens in the case of suppression. If the suppressors keep me below the level "which they have conquered and on the basis of which new conquests will be achieved, then they

---

[243] See also: Yvanka B. Raynova: *Jean-Paul Sartre, A Profound Revision of Husserlian Phenomenology World Wide*, A.-T. Tyminiecka (ed.), *Analecta Husserliana*, vol. 80, Dordrecht/Boston/London: Kluwer Academic Publishers, 2002, p. 323-335.
[244] Simone de Beauvoir, *Force of Circumstance*, p. 75.
[245] Simone de Beauvoir, *The Ethics of Ambiguity*, p. 43.
[246] Sonia Kruks sees in Beauvoir's work the description of a human life, that lacks freedom normally characterizing existence. Beauvoir, so Kruks, develops another notion of the subject than Sartre, because for her the for-itself can be destroyed by the others. For Sartre on the contrary, to diminish existence into in-itself would mean that the suppressed woman would cease to be a human being. Sonia Kruks, Beauvoir: *The Weight of Situation*, in: Elisabeth Fallaize (ed.), *Simone de Beauvoir, A Critical Reader*, p. 61.

are cutting me off from the future, they are changing me into a thing."[247] This however can also happen voluntarily on the basis of an individual project: "the original poverty of his project exempts the sub-man from seeking to legitimize it. He discovers around him only an insignificant and dull world. (...) He cannot prevent himself from being a presence in the world, but he maintains this presence on the plane of bare facticity".[248] In *The Second Sex,* Beauvoir states her standpoint even clearer: "Every time transcendence falls back into immanence, stagnation, there is a degradation of existence into the 'en-soi' – the brutish life of subjection to given conditions – and of liberty into constraint and contingence. This downfall represents a moral fault if the subject consents to it; if it is inflicted upon him, it spells frustrations and oppression. In both cases it is an absolute evil."[249]

In Beauvoir's work freedom is not originating from transcendence as in Sartre's concept of existence, but from the free will. It needs a decision, a will wanting to be a subject. Only by positing myself as a subject and by realizing my concrete projects I will turn myself into a subject, into a transcendence. Otherwise, I remain within immanence, within the in-itself and renounce my freedom. The individual renunciation of freedom represents for Beauvoir a moral lapse, if it is forced onto somebody it leads to frustration and depression. In both cases it is an absolute evil. According to Beauvoir's understanding the human being is

---

[247] Simone de Beauvoir, *The Ethics of Ambiguity*, p. 82.
[248] Ibidem, p. 43.
[249] Simone de Beauvoir, *The Second Sex*, p.XXXV. Here the English translation differs from the French original: "the brutish life of subjection to given conditions" lacks in the French text."

a synthesis of freedom and necessity, transcendence and facticity, being-for-itself and being-in-itself, making it possible that one part, namely freedom-transcendence-being-for-itself, is lost. But is not the whole existentialist approach, which accentuates the impossibility to take only one part of the relation at the cost of the other questioned through that? Can we still speak of a human being if one part of the ambiguity is missing? Can we say that women that live in immanence are still human beings?

Beauvoir is inconsistent in her argumentation. In certain places it seems indeed as if she assumes the loss of being human: when she speaks about "sub-men"[250], about "an absurd vegetation "[251], about the transformation "into a thing ".[252] However, she relativizes this position repeatedly: if man would be allowed to be brute fact, then he would be equal to trees and pebbles, which are not aware that they exist. But the fact is, Beauvoir writes, "that no man is a datum which is passively suffered; the rejection of existence is still another way of existing; nobody can know the peace of the tomb while he is alive."[253] Also concerning the situation of women she points out that every woman is a free and autonomous being like all human creatures"[254] regardless of the situation in which she finds herself. Even if a certain social situation aims at freezing the woman into an object and wanting to condemn her to immanence, she still remains just like every other human being an autonomous freedom. Thus, Beauvoir refers back repeatedly to

---

[250] Simone de Beauvoir, *The Ethics of Ambiguity*, p. 42.
[251] Ibidem, p. 83.
[252] Ibidem, p. 82.
[253] Ibidem, p. 43.
[254] Simone de Beauvoir, *The Second Sex*, p. XXXV.

Sartre's ontology, which excludes a pure being-in-itself for humans. The strain and freedom of being a human can neither be escaped voluntarily nor can one be deprived of it by force.

Beauvoir oscillates between Sartre's position and that of Hegel. Even though Beauvoir criticizes Hegel she does not stop at pure criticism, but partly adopts his ontology. In *The Philosophy of Right* Hegel differentiates between women and men as follows: "Thus one sex (the man, S.M.) is mind in its self-diremption into explicit personal self-subsistence and the knowledge and volition of free universality (...). The other sex (the woman, S.M.) is mind maintaining itself in unity as knowledge and volition in the form of concrete individuality and feeling. In relation to externality the former is powerful and active, the latter passive and subjective. It follows that man has his actual substantive life in the state (...), as well as in labour and struggle with the external world. (...) Woman, on the other hand, has her substantive destiny in the family, and to be imbued with family piety is her ethical frame of mind."[255] Beauvoir follows this classification of Hegel in order to pinpoint how women were turned into the 'other sex' by men: men "have presumed to create a feminine domain – the kingdom of life, of immanence – only in order to lock up women therein."[256] At the same time, she adopts Hegel's concept, to classify all activities involving life itself and its preservation as immanence and being-in-itself. Motherly activities are in Beauvoir's opinion not activities but natural func-

---

[255] G.W.F. Hegel, *Philosophy of Right*, §166, p. 59.
[256] Simone de Beauvoir, *The Second Sex*, p. 65.

tions: "no project is involved".[257] The same goes for household duties and other reproduction activities: they retain the woman within the repetition and the immanence.

Thus, the human being in Beauvoir's eyes is not automatically freedom and transcendence. Rather the individual, as well as the collective will, is needed in order to set oneself as freedom and transcendence by realizing certain projects.

The Liberation to Freedom: the Ethical Dimension of Transcendence in the Work of Simone de Beauvoir

Sartre claims that every human being is free, that it does not even have the possibility to not be free. Beauvoir asks if it is therefore not a contradiction to regard freedom as something conquerable, when it is a priori a given. What sense can there be in the words "to *will oneself* free", since at the beginning we *are* free?[258]

Beauvoir does agree with Sartre that every man/woman is free from the onset, inasmuch as he/she spontaneously casts himself/herself into the world. Every human spontaneity projects itself toward something. This is the case even with failure and neurotic attacks. Beauvoir uses an example to illustrate this directionless spontaneity. It is comparable with a sudden, arbitrary change of direction of an atom in the Epicurean system, "it was necessary for the atom to arrive somewhere. But this movement was not justified by this result which had not been chosen. It remained ab-

---

[257] Ibidem, p. 63.
[258] Simone de Beauvoir, *The Ethics of Ambiguity*, p. 24.

surd."[259] Only if spontaneity is determined by a certain end, it escapes the absurdity of freedom. "My project is never founded; it founds itself."[260] In order to convert spontaneity, which Beauvoir regards as "a vain living palpitation"[261] and as a flight, into a positive project, the will is needed. A decision is necessary, to found the original spontaneity in a project: "Then, by a single movement, my will, establishing the content of the act, is legitimized by it."[262] This means to effect the transition from nature to morality.[263]

Here Beauvoir develops a completely different concept of freedom to Sartre's one. In Sartre's concept freedom originates from transcendence not from will. Sartre emphasizes that the will is "not a privileged manifestation of freedom, but that it is a psychic event of a peculiar structure."[264] It constitutes itself on the same plane as other psychic events and is "supported, neither more nor less than others, by an original, ontological freedom."[265] Sartre points out that we are thrown into the world and realize our projects without having first subjected them to reflection or, respectively, having set them by free will. He develops the concept of the pre-reflective cogito, a consciousness which does not set itself.[266] The will, according to Sartre appears only at the reflexive level; and the goal of a for-itself, that exists according to the will-modus, is to win it-

---

[259] Ibidem, p. 25.
[260] Ibidem, p. 26.
[261] Ibidem, p. 25.
[262] Ibidem, p. 26.
[263] Ibidem, p. 25.
[264] Jean-Paul Sartre, *Being and Nothingness*, p. 452.
[265] Ibidem, p.452.
[266] Ibidem, p. l.

self back, from which a satisfying verdict can be spoken: "I have done what I wished to do."[267] However, the question arises, of where the goals come from if they were not set by the will. *Being and Nothingness* ultimately runs directly toward this topic with growing tension which – according to Sartre – can only be answered through existentialist psychoanalysis, since this would help to uncover the initial project, that being the basis of all other projects.[268]

Beauvoir, on the other hand, believes in the freedom of will and in its central meaning for freedom itself.[269] It is the will which determines the content of my actions and founds my projects. It is will that turns "natural freedom" into "moral freedom."[270] "To will oneself free is to effect the

---

[267] Ibidem, p.452.

[268] Ibidem, p.464.

[269] In her memoirs she writes: "I believe in our freedom, our responsibility, but whatever their importance, this dimension of our existence eludes description. What can be described is merely our conditioning." Simone de Beauvoir, *Force of Circumstance,* p. 6.

[270] Francis Jeanson, in his work *Le problème moral et la pensée de Sartre*, Paris: Editions du Seuil 1947, mentions the fundamental human ambiguity in Sartre's work and explicitly distinguishes between an "attitude naturelle" and an "attitude morale"(p. 31): the freedom that we are condemned to, first has to become "ours"; despite of "free", we have to „liberate" ourselves beforehand, despite of "human", we first have to become "human". p. 27–28. It seems that Jeanson, was influenced by Simone de Beauvoir, who had already been working in 1945 on *The Ethics of Ambiguity* and who Jeanson had been communicating with on an intensive intellectual basis. Her essay was published in the beginning of 1947 in *Les Temps Modernes* to which just as Beauvoir, Jeanson had been also contributing. Apparently, Jeanson did not only adapt relevant notions from Beauvoir's essay but he was furthermore inspired by her to write his book without however giving her any credit for it. His book was published in 1947 and was according to Editions du Seuil (see cover) also

transition from nature to morality by establishing a genuine freedom on the original upsurge of our existence."[271] Nevertheless, one can escape from the will for freedom: "We have said", Beauvoir points out, "that it would be contradictory deliberately to will oneself not free. But one can choose not to will himself free."[272]

In Sartre's work, it would be possible that one can renounce freedom, because that would in itself be an expression of freedom. Sartre allows us to desire to flee from the fears of freedom. He answers the probing question of why we should not be unauthentic by saying, "There is no reason why you should not".[273] Beauvoir responds to this problem of free rejection of freedom by asserting that freedom "cannot establish a denial of itself, for in denying itself, it would deny the possibility of any foundation."[274] Freedom in Beauvoir's work has a very central task which deviates from Sartre's concept: to legitimize the 'per se' meaningless existence. "The man who seeks to justify his life must want freedom itself absolutely and above everything else."[275] Answering the question of what would force man to try to justify his being, Beauvoir says that this is "playing upon the notion of freedom in a dishonest way."[276] The believer is also free to sin; he is tied to the

---

written in the same year, in 1947. I received this information thanks to Yvanka B. Raynova.

[271] Simone de Beauvoir, *The Ethics of Ambiguity*, p. 25.

[272] Ibidem, p. 25.

[273] Jean-Paul Sartre, *Existentialism and Humanism*, Reading, Berkshire: Cox & Wyman 1973, p. 51.

[274] Simone de Beauvoir, *The Ethics of Ambiguity*, p. 24.

[275] Ibidem, p. 24.

[276] Ibidem, p. 16.

divine laws only at the moment he decides to save his soul. Therefore, "a life which does not seek to ground itself will be a pure contingency. But it is permitted to wish to give itself a meaning and a truth, and it then meets rigorous demands within its own heart."[277] Man is free, but in his freedom he finds "his law"[278]: he must assume his freedom "by a constructive movement"[279] and by rejecting oppression for him and others. The individualistic ethics of existentialism would therefore not at all lead to anarchy of personal whim[280], rather it would be "the only proposition of salvation which one can address to men."[281] To be sure of one's ends, no guarantee from outside is necessary. "If it came to be that each man did what he must, existence would be saved in each one without there being any need of dreaming of a paradise where all would be reconciled in death."[282] With this sentence Beauvoir's essay on ethics ends. It reveals how much she was at this point in time still tied to traditional philosophy, especially to Kant, but also to her Christian heritage. It is from these that she tries to find solutions for those problems emerging within the existentialist approach. That Beauvoir had recognized the failure of her efforts can be seen by the sharp criticism to which she later subjected *The Ethics of Ambiguity*. At the same time, this essay reveals a prevailing atmosphere which threads its way throughout Beauvoir's entire life and work. The belief in her will, the clearness and security regarding

---

[277] Ibidem, p. 16.
[278] Ibidem, p. 156.
[279] Ibidem, p. 156.
[280] Ibidem, p. 156.
[281] Ibidem, p. 159.
[282] Ibidem, p. 159.

her own goals accompanied her from childhood to old age. Whereas Sartre connotes the ideal of the will negatively, as man's attempt to try to retain himself and therewith to be God through contentedly judging his own doings – "I have done what I wished to do"[283], for Beauvoir the will represents the pivotal moment in which she finds not only satisfaction but also justification. Here too, Beauvoir's ambiguity is apparent: this security must not only be accompanied by permanent self-criticism but also by a scrutiny of all that which is reputed to be sure and unequivocal. The "ambiguity of his will" must be made apparent, thus "arresting the imperious drive of his subjectivity" in order to question the unconditioned value of the goal."[284]

It may seem that Beauvoir, rather than Sartre, follows the classical German philosophical tradition, but this conclusion would lead to distortion and danger of misinterpretation. Even the conclusion of Beauvoirs essay *The Ethics of Ambiguity* which contains the request to do what one "should" do, including the idea "that the result is not external to the good will which fulfils itself in aiming at it,"[285] should be interpreted existentially despite its obvious dependence and reference to Kant's "Good Will"[286] and its moral "Should". Because this will, which creates the ends "with certainty," owes its meaning not to reason, as with Kant, but rather to a passionate desire: "any man who has known real loves, real revolts, real desires, and real will knows quite well that he has no need of any outside guaran-

---

[283] Jean-Paul Sartre, *Being and Nothingness,* p.452.
[284] Simone de Beauvoir, *The Ethics of Ambiguity*, p. 154.
[285] Ibidem, p. 159.
[286] Ibidem, p. 97. Beauvoir speaks here explicitly of the "men of good will".

tee to be sure of his goals.".[287] Beauvoir wants a human being made out of flesh and blood, someone who is full of passion, as she points out impressively in her early novel *All Men are Mortal*. In *The Ethics of Ambiguity* Beauvoir enforces this viewpoint by claiming those as inferior, as sub-men, "who are denuded of this living warmth – the tepidity which the Gospel speaks of"[288], who feel neither love nor desire[289] and who reject the "passion" which is the human condition; who reject the laceration and failure of that drive toward being which always misses its goal.[290]

It is a great challenge to interpret Beauvoir. Like a fish, she dives into the most varied waters, be it Descartes, Nietzsche, Kierkegaard, Husserl, Kant, Hegel, Marx, be it the differing interpretations that were available to her. But again and again it becomes clear that all these waters obtain their primary colours from existentialism, even if it is not initially apparent.

Beauvoir's concept of the "transition from nature to morality", however, stands completely in the tradition of classical German philosophy. It is characteristic of the Kantian and Hegelian philosophies of freedom that nature has to be overcome and left behind by the transition from nature to morality. In Kant's work, for example, nature is in no way disposed to making life for man as agreeable as possible. Out of the painful knowledge that the human being cannot be seen as the last end of a benevolent and protective nature, the self assurance and self-confidence arises, that man

---

[287] Ibidem, p. 159
[288] Ibidem, p. 42.
[289] Ibidem, p. 42.
[290] Ibidem, p. 42.

has to be his own end, setting his goals as a free actor. According to Kant, only what we do not just do, but do independently from nature gives us a value. It is culture that raises us a natural creature to a rational creature being a worthy, self judging, autonomous participant in the realm of ends.[291] Beauvoir does not explicitly work out the concepts of nature and morality, nevertheless she repeatedly gives us hints at what she understands morality to be. In one instance, she describes true morality as residing "in the painfulness of an indefinite questioning."[292] The value of an act lies, as Kant would say "not in its *conformity* to an external model, but in its internal truth."[293] Then again, she emphasizes that, "in order to make itself effective, morality must not follow the easy way but on the contrary must choose freely the difficult one."[294] The proximity of her concept of morality to the Stoic duty-ideal and to Kant is sometimes astonishing, as the image of the battle against inner and outer resistance is awakened again and again. By calling for the triumph of freedom over facticity, morality demands that the oppressors be suppressed. But on the other hand she emphasizes in quite an existentialist manner that "morality requires that the combatant be not blinded by the goal which he sets up for himself to the point of falling into the fanaticism of seriousness or passion"[295].

Beauvoir's entire essay is written with the intention of pinpointing the ambiguity of the human being in an exis-

---

[291] Immanuel Kant, *The Critique of Judgement*, Oxford: Clarendon Press 1928.
[292] Simone de Beauvoir, *The Ethics of Ambiguity*, p. 133.
[293] Ibidem, p. 138.
[294] Ibidem, p. 154.
[295] Ibidem, p. 89.

tentialist way. Nevertheless she adheres in her argumentation partly to the classical hierarchy between nature and culture.[296] In order to better demonstrate the tension between nature and culture in Beauvoir's work the problem of childhood, denominated by her explicitly as a "natural" situation, shall be examined in the following.

Freedom as a Developmental Process: The Problem of childhood

According to Beauvoir, Descartes had already asserted that man's unhappiness is due to his having first been a child.[297] For a child human inventions, words, customs and values are given facts as inevitable as the sky and the trees; this is to say, "that the world in which he lives is a serious world, since the characteristic of the spirit of seriousness is to consider values as ready-made things."[298] The child lives in a world structured by clear rules and a pre-assigned order. He/she is under the protection of his/her parents and of guardian angels of God. This in turn guarantees security and protection. Nonetheless, the time will come when the adolescent will start posing questions to himself/herself and recognize that humans are not godly and the reality surrounding them has human qualities. Suddenly, he is confronted with having been cast into a world, "which is no

---

[296] Judith Butler holds this opinion, too: "Despite my own previous efforts to argue the contrary, it appears that Beauvoir maintains the mind/body dualism, even as she proposes a synthesis of those terms." Judith Butler, *Gender Trouble*, p. 17.
[297] Simone de Beauvoir, *The Ethics of Ambiguity*, p. 35.
[298] Ibidem, p. 35.

longer ready-made, which has to be made; (...) Freedom is then revealed and he must decide upon his attitude in the face of it."[299] The decisions and the initial project derived from this has consequences for the remainder of one's entire life.

Beauvoir, like Descartes, sees the reason for the unhappiness of man in his first having been a child. The child is shaped by the world that surrounds him, a world where at first his freedom is concealed, providing him with support and safety just because the demands of freedom are still unknown, a world he/she will wish back throughout his entire life. In her *Memoirs of a Dutiful Daughter* Beauvoir illustrates how important it was for her to be confined within a framework whose rigidity would justify her existence. "I realized this because I was afraid of change."[300] She felt that she was one with everything: "we all had our place just here, now, and forever."[301] The orders given by her parents held for her absolute legitimacy and provided the framework for her feeling sheltered in an intact world.

Beauvoir sees the absolute necessity in attending to the child: "he needs to be taken in hand, he invites authority, it is the form which the resistance of facticity, through which all liberation is brought about, takes for him."[302] Childhood which forms the base for the developing personality of the human being thus either does not dispose of freedom altogether or only as a random freedom. "This contingency recalls, in a way, the arbitrariness of the grace distributed

---

[299] Ibidem, p. 39.
[300] Simone de Beauvoir, *Memoirs of a Dutiful Daughter*, p. 62.
[301] Ibidem, p. 80.
[302] Simone de Beauvoir, *The Ethics of Ambiguity*, p. 141.

by God in Calvinistic doctrine. Here too there is a sort of predestination issuing not from an external tyranny, but from the operation of the subject itself."[303]

Childhood represents a common and temporary "*natural situation*"[304] for all humans, natural due to the fact that its limitations were not created by other people. Therefore it cannot be compared with a situation created by man through suppression. However, according to Beauvoir, there are people that remain in a childlike world throughout their entire life; which is the case for slaves that have not yet become aware of their slavery, as well as for women, who in many cultures have no other possibility but to "submit to the laws, the gods, the customs, and the truths created by the males."[305] Ignorance and making mistakes are unchangeable facts just like the walls of a prison. The African slave of the 18th century, as well as the Muslim woman imprisoned in a harem have no means to strike back against a suppressive culture. These enforced situations have to be separated from those situations that enable free choice. According to Beauvoir, the modern woman of the Western world chooses her situation or is at least in agreement with it.[306] Already in *The Ethics of Ambiguity* Beauvoir does not see the situation of the woman as a "natural" one. Being a woman is therefore not the consequence of a female nature that has to be accepted as a given one. Beauvoir adheres to this concept further in the second part of *The Second Sex* which she calls "lived experience",

---

[303] Ibidem, p. 41.
[304] Ibidem, p. 141.
[305] Ibidem, p. 37.
[306] Ibidem, p. 38.

where she separates the "situation" of the woman from her "development". Not to be born as a woman but to become one points to the fact that we are born into this world as children. Childhood represents a "natural" situation, womanhood however is something that had been introduced by humans themselves. Womanhood always implies a choice. To which extent the "suppressive culture" pre-assigns women's projects and thus their choice, however, is not yet addressed in *The Ethics of Ambiguity*. Nevertheless, Beauvoir points out in a general way, that the freedom of the individual is only guaranteed through the freedom of all. In order to be able to lead one's life in freedom it is necessary to fight for the liberation of society in its entirety.

The "serious" man however decides consciously to live in a childlike world. He negates his freedom in favor of his absolute goals. According to Beauvoir the reason for this can be seen not as much in the fear of freedom, but rather in the remaining desire for the lost state of childhood. After one has been promised divinity and has lived under God's eyes in one's childhood, one is not inclined to simply be a man again with all his restlessness and doubts. The "serious" man is convinced that by confirming these values he will attain permanent value for himself: "Shielded with 'rights', he fulfills himself as a *being* who is escaping from the stress of existence."[307]

Whereas Sartre considers inauthenticity and seriousness as being effects of fear that he in turn connects ontologically to freedom, Beauvoir adds a historical aspect.[308] Seri-

---

[307] Ibidem, p. 46.
[308] See: Debra Bergoffen, *Bad Faith as History*, in: Debra Bergoffen, *The Philosophy of Simone de Beauvoir*, p. 82.

ousness is not only the fear of freedom itself, but rather the desire for childhood during which all wishes had been fulfilled in an unambiguous way. Thus, seriousness would therefore not so much be a symptom of refusing to combat my fear of freedom, but rather that others succeed in conserving me in the state of childhood. It is no coincidence that slaves have been compared to children. The slave is, just like a child, unaware of the fact that the world is constituted and not given. In this way, Beauvoir writes in *The Ethics of Ambiguity* that women often develop "childish qualities which are forbidden to adults because they are based on a feeling of irresponsibility".[309]

Thus, Beauvoir equates childhood with a state of being-in-itself where the awareness of freedom, of being-for-itself, has not yet been discovered and recognized and where freedom is to be found either by chance or not at all. The development during childhood is called by Beauvoir "natural history"[310] in reference to the naturalness of the life of a child. Only during adolescence is moral decision making attained, which however is free" and therefore unforeseeable."[311]

Beauvoir adheres to Hegel's approach, who emphasizes in the *Phenomenology of the Spirit*: "Though the embryo is indeed *in itself* a human being, it is not so *for itself*; this it only is as cultivate Reason, which has *made* itself into what it is *in itself*."[312] For Hegel being-in-itself implies the potentiality, the possibility of being a human, just as the seed

---

[309] Simone de Beauvoir, *The Ethics of Ambiguity*, p. 37.
[310] Ibidem, p. 39.
[311] Ibidem, p. 40.
[312] G.W.F. Hegel, *Phenomenology of Spirit*, p. 12.

carries the possibility for becoming a tree. The child is a human being inasmuch as he/she carries in himself/herself the potentiality of being a human, however in reality his/her being human has not yet been fully realized. Consequently he/she is not confronted yet with the rights and duties of an adult human being. If the child becomes a man/woman he/she will be able to realize himself/herself as a human being. However, in Hegel's work this does not include the woman to the same extent as the man. For Hegel, "the difference in the physical characteristics of the two sexes has a rational basis and consequently acquires an intellectual and ethical significance."[313] Therefore the woman is limited to the area connected with the family which only allows for a partial realization of her being a human. Even though man can fail in realizing his freedom as well, for instance in remaining dependent upon earned income and thus dependent upon others and not free in hisr existence, there remains the possibility of at least escaping this state. For the woman however, there is no such possibility due to her nature in connection with her destination within the family. The destination of the woman thus stands in opposition to the destination of the human being itself. The destination of the man in contrast is in accordance with the destination of the human being. Considering this Hegelian concept, it becomes evident why Beauvoir writes in *The Second Sex* that: "The advantage man enjoys, which makes itself felt from his childhood, is that his vocation as a human being in no way runs counter to his destiny as a male."[314] Beauvoir understands man to be a potential-

---

[313] G.W.F. Hegel, *Philosophy of Right*, §165, p. 59.
[314] Simone de Beauvoir, *The Second Sex*, p. 682.

ity, just as Hegel does, as a being-in-itself, which only through the will for freedom can be set as being-for-itself, as transcendence.

Beauvoir obviously makes a distinction between situations and "natural" situations. This classification deviates largely from Sartre's position who – as we saw before – assumes that it is impossible to grasp facticity in its "brute nudity", since all we will find is already "recovered and freely constructed".[315] Beauvoir adheres to this concept concerning women, however apparently not concerning children, whereby it becomes possible for her to address a kind of in-itself-stage "before" having entered freedom, before having become a for-itself. At the same time, she closely relates the topic of women again and again to childhood, either by arguing that women have often been treated like children or that in turn that they behave as such, or by comparing oppression with retaining someone in the stage of childhood, presenting things to them as naturally given and unchangeable. In *The Second Sex,* Beauvoir points out that the woman is condemned to stay an "eternal child".[316] Thus, she uses different and contradicting arguments when referring to childhood. On the one hand, childhood symbolizes the search for a lost paradise, where everything has its place and order, and on the other hand she portrays it as a place of "perdition", where freedom is either not present at all or present only by chance.

This almost leads to the conclusion that freedom had chased us away from the blissfulness of paradise and that we are now condemned to being free. Beauvoir seems to be

---

[315] J.-P Sartre, *Being and Nothingness,* p. 83.
[316] Simone de Beauvoir, *The Second Sex*, p. 598.

well aware of this contradiction when she contrasts happiness with freedom in the introduction to the Second Sex, taking freedom as the only principle for ethics: "those who are condemned to stagnation are often pronounced happy on the pretext that happiness consists in being at rest. This notion we reject."[317] The topic of childhood appears to be a problematic one from yet another viewpoint. On the one hand, Beauvoir takes a very strict position concerning freedom: "once there appears a possibility of liberation, it is resignation of freedom not to exploit the possibility, a resignation which implies dishonesty and which is a positive fault".[318] On the other hand, she relativizes this position again whenever she is referring to children because: "the freedom of the parents would be ruin of their sons, and as freedom and the future are on the side of the latter, these are the ones who must first be taken into account".[319] Beauvoir addresses here quite calmly and without further comment one of the biggest problems facing feminism. Does this mean that parents have to refrain from their own freedom in favor of their children? Is the emancipation concept proposed by Beauvoir valid only for women and men without children? For, the liberation of women is inevitably connected to children themselves and has consequences for them. This would result in the claim not to bear children anymore and to reject motherhood altogether. Is this however, the solution for the encountered problems and does this help women?

---

[317] Ibidem, p. XXXIV.
[318] Simone de Beauvoir, *The Ethics of Ambiguity*, p. 38.
[319] Ibidem, p. 143.

Being and Failure

Beauvoir explores the question as to how the inevitable failure that is linked with the realization of concrete projects can be overcome. Goals represent an integral aspect of a project. Without a goal there is no project. Already in *Pyrrhus et Cinéas* Beauvoir committed herself to the paradox of the goal: on the one hand, a goal must be posited as absolute, it must be pursued seriously; on the other hand, once it is reached it is immediately transcended and therefore relativized. In *The Ethics of Ambiguity* this problem is expanded by the dimension of freedom. In fact, the goal is still an integral aspect of the project, but freedom becomes more significant. Goals must still be pursued, but they are no longer allowed to be posited as absolute. Rather, in reference to Husserl, they should be put "in parentheses", whereby they are, as in an electric circuit that has been suspended, still present, but have lost their effectiveness. Beauvoir is looking for a way out of the failure, which is connected with man's initial project, namely the desire to be. Thus, according to Beauvoir, public opinion rightfully admires a man "who, having been ruined or having suffered an accident, knows how to gain the upper hand, that is, how to renew his engagement in the world, thereby strongly asserting the independence of freedom."[320]

However, this requires that, despite obstacles and disappointments, one retains free disposition over one's future and that the situation offers new possibilities. Therefore, the most abhorrent punishments are those that force the

---

[320] Simone de Beauvoir, *The Ethics of Ambiguity*, p. 29.

human being to actions that are devoid of sense, such as senselessly digging up the same ditch or copying the same sentence again and again. Solitary confinement is the most abominable punishment, because it sustains the facticity of being, but denies the possibility of justification: "A freedom cannot will itself without willing itself as an indefinite movement. It must absolutely reject the constraints which arrest its drive toward itself." [321] One is justified in using violence against these constraints if this opens up concrete possibilities to the freedom which one is trying to preserve.[322] Beauvoir emphasizes repeatedly that it is by his project that man fulfills himself, "by the end at which he aims that he justifies himself; thus, this justification is always to come."[323] In *The Second Sex* she formulates the problem as follows: "There is no justification for present existence other than its expansion into an indefinitely open future".[324]

Beauvoir proposes a way out of failure by developing the concept of the existentialist conversion.[325] According to Husserl's phenomenological reduction the will to be is "put in parentheses" which does not mean that my drive, my wishes, my projects or my sufferings are suspended, but rather that the possibility of failure can be avoided by refusing to set up as absolutes the goals toward which my transcendence thrusts itself and to consider them in connection with the freedom which projects them.[326] According to Beauvoir there is a direct kind of attachment to being

---

[321] Ibidem, p. 31.
[322] Ibidem, p. 137.
[323] Ibidem, p. 115.
[324] Simone de Beauvoir, *The Second Sex*, p. XXXV.
[325] Simone de Beauvoir, *The Ethics of Ambiguity*, p. 13.
[326] Ibidem, p. 14.

which is not the relationship "wanting to be", but rather "wanting to disclose being".[327] This disclosure of being allows keeping a distance from it, to not have to appropriate it, to not want to possess it: "I cannot appropriate the snow field where I slide. It remains foreign, forbidden, but I take delight in this very effort toward an impossible possession. I experience it as a triumph, not as a defeat."[328] Beauvoir looks for a way out of the useless of passion man wanting to be God: "man, in his vain attempt to *be* God, makes himself exist *as* man."[329] However, this disclosure implies a perpetual tension, that of keeping oneself at a certain distance, tearing oneself from the world, and asserting oneself as a freedom: "To wish for the disclosure of the world and to assert oneself as freedom are one and the same movement. Freedom is the source from which all significations and all values spring."[330]

So what is it that Beauvoir wants to accomplish?

Beauvoir attempts to create an existentialist ethics based on Sartre's *Being and Nothingness*, whereby she departs from the ambivalence of Sartre's 'initial project'. On the one hand we must strive for being; we are forced to engage ourselves, to provide ourselves with an identity, which means to choose ourselves. On the other hand we should become aware that the being we are striving for is unattainable, because due to our ontological structure we are never, as is the case for things, in accordance with ourselves, that is we can never have the identity of an in-itself. If we re-

---

[327] Ibidem, p. 12.
[328] Ibidem, p. 12.
[329] Ibidem, p. 12.
[330] Ibidem, p. 24.

cognize, firstly, that we must choose ourselves again and again, and secondly, that it is us who through our choices assign a certain meaning and value to things, then we turn against the spirit of seriousness, assigning things a value independently of man's existence. Existentialism turns against fixed identity-forming attributes that attempt to define man once and for all; as in the case of Genet[331], who through one petty theft is forever defined as a thief; or in the case of blacks, Jews, or women, where it is claimed that certain characteristics can be objectively defined through the colour of skin or bodily endowments. Beauvoir's concept of the existentialist conversion builds upon our ability to disclose being, on our freedom; it constitutes the origin and the pre-condition of a possible liberation recognizing that we must constantly engage ourselves anew to give things a meaning and thus to disclose being and our own existence.

Debra Bergoffen interprets Beauvoir to the effect that Beauvoir had developed two essentially different approaches to being, which are based on different understandings of intentionality. Beauvoir, according to Bergoffen, "newly" describes the "dynamic of intentionality" and combines the ontology of existentialism with an ethics that is based on "the joy of existence and the moral value of generosity".[332] She contrasts "the ethics of the project", dominated by the "will to be" with "the ethics of the epoché" that would "validate the will that delights in letting being show itself – a will with no desire to appropriate the

---

[331] Jean-Paul Sartre, *Saint Genet, Actor and Martyr*, New York: Braziller, 1963.
[332] Debra Bergoffen, *The Philosophy of Simone de Beauvoir*, p. 76.

object it reveals".[333] Bergoffen claims that in Beauvoir's work intentionality can be seen as comprising two moments: a moment that discloses being, and a moment that identifies the disclosing "I" with the being it discloses. According to Bergoffen, Beauvoir's account of the first intentional moment echoes Husserl and Merleau-Ponty. In this moment I unveil the meanings of being, experience myself as freedom of revelation, and am aware that the intersubjective world is the nexus of my life. Beauvoir's account of the second intentional moment echoes Hegel and Sartre, here I appropriate the disclosed meanings of being by insisting on the my-ness of the being I disclose. Bergoffen sees in the contesting bond of these two moments the reason for Beauvoir's ambiguity of the human condition and the source of her unique philosophical perspective. Here is not the place to discuss Bergoffen's interpretation of Sartre and Hegel, but rather to look at the consequences we can draw from the above. By considering the will of being equal to the will of the project, Bergoffen interprets that Beauvoir had wanted to put the will of the project in parentheses and had propagated only the will of disclosure. Thus Bergoffen sees the project defined as setting and chasing a goal, generally, as an instrument of mastery and appropriation, contesting the position of disclosure rooted in a basic mood of joy, generosity and erotics. This leads Bergoffen to the conclusion that Beauvoir had based her ethics of liberation on this disclosure and its fundamental mood – joy. Thus Beauvoir had written: "in order for the

---

[333] Ibidem, p. 93.

idea of liberation to have a concrete meaning, the joy of existence must be asserted in each one, at every instant."[334]

What would this approach mean for the liberation of women?

In *The Second Sex* Beauvoir insists that woman must try to attain access to the world and to society. She must not seek her individual salvation in love or mysticism but has to cast herself into the world through the realization of her projects. Only when this stage has been reached, which usually has been denied to women, would Beauvoir consider it desirable to let generosity prevail. The aspect of generosity already plays an important role in Beauvoir's *Pyrrhus et Cinéas* – long before Sartre included it in his *Notebooks of an Ethics* as a relevant aspect of ethics – Beauvoir's regret can be anticipated about men having made this world a world of fight and conflict. However, it is far fetched to claim that Beauvoir made way in her design of the project for an ethics of generosity, eroticism and love. Furthermore, it would miss Beauvoir's initial intention altogether in that the subject has to set himself/herself concretely through his/her projects. Beauvoir rather emphasizes starting with *Pyrrhus et Cinéas* right up until *The Ethics of Ambiguity* and *The Second Sex* her ethics of the project by attaching increasing expectations to the project. In *The Second Sex* all activities that involve only sustaining and propagation of the species are excluded even if they are connected with joy and happiness. Already at the beginning of *The Second Sex* she contrasts the ethics of happiness with that of liberation knowing that both easily conflict

---

[334] Ibidem, p. 101.

with one another and that the ethics of liberation requires certain contributions.

Beauvoir does not speak out for a purely aesthetic lifestyle, although it is precisely the example of the snow-covered field, rendering joy without the desire to possess it, which provokes this impression. This would be entirely against her basic ethical intention. Beauvoir does not stop at the disclosure of being, which she understands as precondition and as the starting point for a theory of liberation, but rather she demands an active engagement for a concrete liberation. The disclosure of being makes it possible to acquire an awareness of our freedom, thus enabling the rejection of the strategy of the oppressors fraudulently portraying oppression as "a natural situation since, after all, one cannot revolt against nature."[335]

---

[335] Simone de Beauvoir, *The Ethics of Ambiguity*, p. 83.

Part II
Subject, Society, Recognition

Recognition between Conflict and Reciprocity

The concept of freedom in Beauvoir's work is closely connected to the problem of recognition. Beauvoir develops her concept of recognition in different steps, beginning with the problem of the relation to the Other. In her diaries dating from the year 1927 she emphasizes for the first time the significance of the relation to the Other: "I must rework my philosophical ideas (...) go deeper into the problems that have appealed to me (...). The theme is almost always this opposition of self and Other that I have felt since beginning to live."[336]

In *She Came to Stay,* her first published novel, the topic of recognition assumes the focal point of Beauvoir's interest. Departing from Hegel's thesis that each consciousness wants the death of the Other, Beauvoir emphasizes the conflict with the Other and the difficulty of reciprocal recognition. Whereas, she had still considered the conflict with the Other as an irresolvable problem in this novel published in 1943 only the death of the rival seems to be an escape from the dilemma of mutual claims, in her following works she is seeking a new approach towards the Other. In her novel *The Blood of Others,* written towards the end of the War

---

[336] Margaret A. Simons, *Beauvoir's Early Philosophy: The 1927 Diary (1998)*, in: *Beauvoir and the Second Sex, Feminism, Race, an dthe Origins of Existentialism*, Boston: Rowman & Littlefield 1999, p. 217.

and published in 1945, she emphasizes the responsibility for each. Just as in the ethics of *The Ethics of Ambiguity*, published in 1947, it is now required that one takes a stand and commits oneself to active involvement. Reflecting on her past Beauvoir describes this development in her memoirs *The Prime of Life* in a strikingly critical manner.[337] From her youth onwards, she writes, she had refused to admit that life contained any will other than her own: "I refused to envisage other people as potential individuals, with consciences, like myself."[338] From this position the existence of Other remained a danger for her, one which she could not bring herself to face openly: "I fought hard against sorcery that aimed to turn me into a monster, and I was still on the defensive."[339]

Later on, she reminisces and states: "It is impossible to assign any particular day, week, or even month to the conversation that took place in me about this time. (...) I renounced my individualistic, anti-humanistic way of life. I learned the value of solidarity."[340] History had seized her. Ideas, values, everything was overthrown. Instead of her previous idealist view of the world she developed a stronger accentuation of our being situated in a particular place, as well as the historical conditioning of the human being, on which she comments in her memoirs:"In truth, society has been all about me from the day of my birth; it is in the bosom of that society, and in my own close relation-

---

[337] Simone de Beauvoir, *The Prime of Life*, p. 91.
[338] Ibidem, p. 127.
[339] Ibidem, p. 125.
[340] Ibidem, p. 359.

ship with it, that all my personal decisions must be formed."[341]

However the systematic examination of the problem of the Other in connection with the topic of recognition is only performed in her main work, *The Second Sex,* with an entirely new approach, namely that of gender relations: women, in opposition to men, now become the embodiment of the Other in general, which leads to the renunciation of their being recognized as subjects. Herein, Beauvoir places the problem of the Other into an entirely new and different context than Sartre, who had addressed this topic in detail in *Being and Nothingness*. This way Beauvoir's originality and autonomy becomes apparent in that she develops a completely new concept of the Other in connection with gender relations. Whereas Beauvoir had still assumed in her earlier works that an individual only achieves a human dimension through being recognized by the Other, accentuating the individual-psychological side of recognition, she later came to the conclusion that the situation of women is determined in a specific manner by a process of recognition within society. Thus, she expanded the topic of recognition beyond the private towards the public sphere and the problem of gender relations.

Beauvoir's discussion of the topic of recognition and the relation to the Other is thus subject to constant development and transformation. Similarly, as in the case of the concept of freedom, a transformation from an individual towards a societal and practice-oriented view takes place. However, some basic concepts, which are elaborated in her earlier works, are essential to the understanding of *The*

---

[341] Ibidem, p. 550.

Second Sex and are therefore reflected on in the text to follow.

She Came to Stay

In her novel *She Came to Stay*, which was started in October 1938 and completed by early summer 1941, Beauvoir reflected on her personal experience of a passionate ménage à trois with Olga Kosakievicz[342] and her long-term companion Jean Paul Sartre, which had started in 1933 and culminated in 1937.[343] In this novel Beauvoir's specific approach to philosophy becomes manifest, as well as the importance she attributes to personal experience. In her memoirs she expresses how philosophy represents for her a living reality, an unstoppable source for her own life and her experiences: "If a theory convinced me, it did not remain an external, alien phenomenon; it altered my relationship with the world, and colored all my experience."[344] She was not so much interested in building up a philosophical system from which new insights for the entire universe could be derived: "as I have remarked before, women are not by nature prone to obsessions of this type."[345] Instead what she wanted was to communicate her personal experience, and this was possible for her mainly in literature.[346] In her novel *She Came to Stay,* Françoise, being representa-

---

[342] Beauvoir explicitly dedicated *She Came to Stay* to Olga Kosakievicz.
[343] See: Claude Francis et Fernande Gontier, *Les Ecrits de Simone de Beauvoir*, Paris: Gallimard 1979, p. 37.
[344] Simone de Beauvoir, *The Prime of Life*, p. 221.
[345] Ibidem, p. 221.
[346] Ibidem, p. 221.

tive of Beauvoir, says the following: "To me, an idea is not a question of theory, (…). It passes the test, or, if it remains theoretical, it has no value. (…) Otherwise, I wouldn't have waited for Xavière's arrival to be certain that my conscience is not unique in this world. ".[347] Whereas at the beginning of the novel, Françoise had adhered to the idea that "Only her own life was real"[348], and that she would have the power to bring life to things[349], thus believing "that she was dominating Xavière, possessing her even in her past and in the still unknown meanderings of her future,"[350] she now found herself confronted with Xavière's stubborn resistance, this obstinate will against which her own will was breaking.

Beauvoir describes Xavière as the person that never confided in anyone, never allowed anyone to come close to her and who insisted stubbornly to remain a stranger.[351] In the midst of utmost desperation she maintained her poise fully. Xavière never gave herself up; even if she positioned the Other high above herself, even if she loved someone, "one remained an object to her".[352] Xavière is depicted here as absolute freedom, as pure negation, as a subject that can never become an object and never gives itself up but rather makes the Other into an object. Thus, she represents the exact opposite of that which Beauvoir will later introduce in *The Second Sex* concerning the situation of the woman,

---

[347] Simone de Beauvoir, *She Came to Stay*, London: Flamingo, Fontana Paperbacks, 1988, p. 302.
[348] Ibidem, p. 2.
[349] Ibidem.
[350] Ibidem, p. 26.
[351] Ibidem, p. 340.
[352] Ibidem, p. 303.

namely of being made into an object and remaining in this state without in turn making man into an object.[353]

Beauvoir succeeds in working out the conflict between two consciousnesses in her novel, not only in a literary way, but also in a philosophical way, based on her own experience.[354] In Hegel's work, to which Beauvoir had dedicated herself intensely from 1940, she found the philosophical theory that explicitly dealt with the antagonism of two consciousnesses in the struggle for recognition. However, in Beauvoir's opinion, Hegel would not stop at that point but would continue the search for a solution of the conflict. Thus, she writes in a letter to Sartre dating back to July 1940, that Hegel, contrary to Sartre, would maintain a certain level of optimism: "There are many analogies, but Hegel allows for the things that are dire and grim in their eyes to transform into joy. And apparently both facts are true and I would like to find a balance"[355].

---

[353] Interpretations like the one from Jane Heath on the contrary identify Xavière "as the locus of the threatening and destabilizing feminine within the text, undermining the masculine economy represented by Pierre and Françoise." Thus the murder of Xavière is interpreted as "phallic backlash, an act of repression of the hysterical feminine undertaken by the masculine-identified Françoise, in the interests of maintaining the phallic order." Jean Heath, *She Came to Stay: The Phallus strikes back*, in: Elizabeth Fallaize (ed.), *Simone de Beauvoir. A Critical Reader*, London-New York: Routledge 1998, p. 171.

[354] Several things seem to indicate that Beauvoir indeed inspired Sartre through her ideas which goes against the belief that Beauvoir – as it had been long assumed – simply had utilized Sartre's theoretical concept in concrete situations – even if it would be far fetched to conclude that Sartre's *Being and Nothingness* represents a mere application of Beauvoir's novel *She Came to Stay*.

[355] Simone de Beauvoir, *Letters to Sartre*, London: Vintage, 1992,

Right from her early works, Beauvoir seems to be attempting to find a way out of the dilemma of mutual claims.

In *She Came To Stay* Beauvoir makes an attempt in this direction. She opposes the destructive encounter of two consciousnesses – those of Xavière and Françoise – with the friendship between Françoise and Pierre. The relation of Françoise and Pierre is explicitly depicted as friendship: both refrain from dominating each other. "The moment you acknowledge my conscience, you know that I acknowledge one in you, too. That makes all the difference."[356] Pierre responds to Françoise's statement that she never had any difficulty with him. Pierre confirms this by emphasizing that there had always been "a give and take between us."[357] Later, in her memoirs *The Prime of Life* Beauvoir remarked: "The existence of Otherness remained a danger for me, and one which I could not bring myself to face openly. (...) I had settled the anomaly of Sartre by telling myself that we formed a single entity."[358] She admits that she had very conveniently persuaded herself for a long time, "that a foreordained harmony existed between us on every single point."[359]

In contrast to Sartre's concept of being-for-others unity and identity thus seem to play a pivotal role in Beauvoir's concept of friendship. Thus, Beauvoir describes Françoise as someone who always felt the need to gain Pierre's approval: "her every thought was with him and for him; an act, self-initiated and having no connection with him, an act

---

Vol.2, p. 198.
[356] Simone de Beauvoir, *She Came to Stay*, p. 303.
[357] Ibidem, p. 302.
[358] Simone de Beauvoir *The Prime of Life*, p. 125.
[359] Ibidem, p. 143.

that bespoke genuine independence, was beyond her imagination. Yet this was not disturbing; she would never find it necessary to fall back on herself in opposition to Pierre."[360] The encounter with Xavière however, taught her in a painful way "that he lived his own life",[361] while she had made the mistake for years of only regarding him as justification for her own existence. Deprived of this security, Françoise now asks herself: "Just what am I?"[362], a question that will preoccupy Beauvoir right up to her later memoirs *All Said and Done*.[363]

Françoise noticed that Pierre claimed a certain independence: "'we are but one': that's all very nice, but Pierre was demanding his independence. Of course, in a sense they were two, this she knew very well."[364] As Pierre's relationship with Xavière developed, Françoise realized that by alienating herself in him, she had lost all sense of her

---

[360] Ibidem, p. 108.
[361] Ibidem, p. 131.
[362] Ibidem, p. 146.
[363] "Why am I myself" (p. 9) she asks here. Although life is determined by an inexhaustible multiplicity of relationships with the world, there is "a center of interiorization, a *me,* which asserts that it is always the same throughout the whole course." (p. 10) she writes in *All Said and Done*. If we cannot say with Sartre that life "is", we nevertheless can ask about what it forms. There have been two factors that have provided the essential unity to her life: the place that Sartre has always had in it, and her faithfulness to her original project – that of knowing and of writing. (p. 38). "My life has been the fulfillment of a primary design; and at the same time it has been the product and the expression of the world in which it developed. That is why in telling it I have been able to speak of a great deal other than myself. (...) But through all my changes I still see myself."(p. 39,40) Simone de Beauvoir, *All Said and Done*, Penguin Books, Harmondsworth 1977.
[364] Simone de Beauvoir, *She Came to Stay*, p. 57.

own identity[365]: she fell into a deep identity-crisis[366]. Even though Beauvoir poses the question as to which extent it is possible to live in unity with others and to still retain one's independence, she does not find a solution: it results in the destruction of the Other, threatening one's identity.

Here we are faced with two distinct forms of recognition. On the one hand, the encounter between two consciousnesses is described as a hostile opposition trying to make the Other into an object in order to be the only subject, nevertheless also being continually threatened to be turned into an object by the Other. This concept is found in Sartre's *Being and Nothingness*: the relation to the Other is always the conflict never leading to mutual reciprocity.[367] Thus, in Beauvoir's novel, published in the same year as Sartre's *Being and Nothingness*, Xavière was considered the prototype of sadism as described by Sartre. The focal point was placed on the destructive relationship between Xavière and Françoise, whereas the aspect of friendship and mutual recognition remained unaddressed. [368]

---

[365] See: Toril Moi, *The Making of an Intellectual Woman*, p. 109.

[366] The way out of this crisis is the murder on Xavière. According to Toril Moi, Françoise had recognized, that her relationship to Pierre was unsound, that the fault was all her own, and that what she needed to do was to affirm her own identity and independence. Beauvoir released Françoise through the agency of a crime, from the dependent position in which her love for Pierre kept her. Toril Moi, *The Making of an Intellectual woman*, p. 110.

[367] Sartre writes: "The essence of the relations between consciousnesses is not the *Mitsein*; it is conflict." Jean-Paul Sartre, *Being and Nothingness*, p. 429.

[368] Toril Moi, for example, interprets this in a psychoanalytic way as murder on the jealous and intrusive mother. Toril Moi, *The Making of an Intellectual Woman*, p. 119.

However, the concept of friendship described in Beauvoir's work poses various problems. On the one hand, the existentialist approach demands separate reflection on concrete individuals, never allowing them to be transcended towards an abstract unity or totality. On the other hand, Beauvoir seems to presuppose in *She Came to Stay,* as well as in her memoirs, an impartial unity as being the precondition for friendship. Mutuality, this means the mutual recognition of two human beings as subjects seems to be a necessary but not a sufficient condition for friendship. Beauvoir speaks in reference to Sartre of a "pact" – a responsibility in a clearly defined role, unlimited trust and similarity between the projects that enable us to take part in the Other's life. Beauvoir regards these attributes as being essential for friendship. The absolute Otherness that cannot be reached by reflection seems to be not only inefficacious for friendship but also it poses a danger that is to be faced even by violent means if needs be. Absolute freedom, which consists of pure negation, refraining from any responsibility only to prove itself as sheer arbitrariness, never knowing what will be decided from moment to moment, is contrasted by Beauvoir with freedom. Freedom includes and recognizes the freedom of the Other and is not only defined by a mutual goal but also implies a contract in the form of a mutual responsibility. Xavière, however, rejects all arguments as being bourgeois and moralist and regards

---

Julie Ward, on the other hand, shows the failure concerning reciprocity and friendship in *She Came to Stay,* Julie Ward, "Reciprocity and Friendship in Beauvoir's Thought", in: *Hypatia. A Journal of Feminist Philosophy*, Vol. 14, Indiana University Press, Bloomington 1999, p. 41.

herself proudly as an amoral being who is only concerned about her freedom.

Thus, Beauvoir elevates friendship to a moral level and pinpoints two extreme poles of possibilities for the encounter with the Other without pointing out that normal daily encounters are generally less spectacular compared to the two extremes of friendship or violence. In *She Came to Stay*, however, Beauvoir contrasts the destructive relationship with Xavière, who rejects any form of morality, with the moral relation of friendship in terms of the mutual recognition occurring between Françoise and Pierre. In *The Ethics of Ambiguity*, Beauvoir values friendship together with charity as being on the level of Kantian morality.[369] However, Beauvoir does not explore further the topic of friendship, neither in this essay nor in *Pyrrhus et Cinéas*. Only in *The Second Sex* does she classify friendship as the highest goal: only within friendship can mutual recognition be realized in practice.[370]

It could be interpreted that the insistence in *She Came to Stay* on absolute freedom and unlimited individual difference is bound to result in conflicts that can only be resolved through the death of the other consciousness. Beauvoir's initial choice for the title for *She Came to Stay*, *Légitime Défense*, which was changed on the advice of the editor to *L'Invitée*, is a further indication of this.[371] Thus, if the Other does not show any further willingness to compromise, the insistence on the Other's death would be a legitimate defence. Therefore, a minimal amount of commonal-

---

[369] Simone de Beauvoir, *The Ethics of Ambiguity*, p. 135.
[370] Simone de Beauvoir, *The Second Sex*, p. 141.
[371] Simone de Beauvoir *The Prime of Life*, p. 519.

ities must exist between both consciousnesses in order to be able to coexist. The moral standpoint seems to be a prerequisite for a successful coexistence. This illustrates that Beauvoir had always been interested into moral questions. Just as she herself points out in an interview with Margaret Simons in 1982, this would illustrate one of the large differences between herself and Sartre: "In the *Second Sex*, I place myself much more on a moral plane whereas Sartre dealt with morality later on. In fact, he never exactly dealt with morality. In *Being and Nothingness*, he's not looking for the moral, he's seeking a description of what existence is. It's more an ontology than a morality".[372] Beauvoir had already attempted a "pluralist morality"[373] in 1929 during a philosophical debate with Sartre. However, as she recollects in her *Memoirs of a Dutiful Daughter,* she was bound to face "that many of my opinions were based only on prejudice, dishonesty, or hastily formed concepts, that my reasoning was a fault and that my ideas were in a muddle"[374], prompting some interpreters of Beauvoir thereafter to draw the conclusion that from there on Beauvoir had felt herself as an inferior philosopher to Sartre, causing her withdrawal from philosophy altogether.[375]

To what extent it is possible to preserve one's individual independence, and to what extent is being different still acceptable? Such questions are raised and addressed by Beauvoir repeatedly in her writing. A tension can be felt

---

[372] Margaret A. Simons, *Beauvoir Interview* (1982) in: Margaret A. Simons, *Beauvoir and the Second Sex*, p. 58.
[373] Simone de Beauvoir, *Memoirs of a Dutiful Daughter*, p. 344.
[374] Ibidem, p. 344.
[375] See: Toril Moi, *The Making of an Intellectual Woman*, p. 16, and Michèle Le Dœueff, *Hipparchia's Choice*, p. 162.

regarding her position on friendship, emerging from the decision for mutual recognition and responsibility, and her position on the project, defined by the freedom to realize deliberately chosen projects, that can conflict with each other. In *Pyrrhus et Cinéas* she writes: "I do not want to be recognized by anyone, because it is through communication with the Other that we attempt to complete our project in which our freedom is involved".[376] How this can be undertaken in the case of individuals, who exist in different situations manifests itself increasingly as a nearly insolvable problem. But even in the *Ethics of Ambiguity* Beauvoir was still convinced that we must not "deny *a priori* that separate existents can, at the same time, be bound to each other, that their individual freedoms can forge laws valid for all."[377] In retrospect, she critizises her early essay: "in my essay, coexistence appears as a sort of accident that each individual should somehow surmount; he should begin by hammering out his "project" in solitary state, and only then ask the masses to endorse its validity, while in truth I am born into society and only in close relationship with it, I can decide what to do."[378] In *The Second Sex* she points out, that the project is not only dependent upon ourselves, nor solely upon the Other that we meet, but upon the general position of a society in respect to individual projects.[379] Already in *The Ethics of Ambiguity* Beauvoir

---

[376] Simone de Beauvoir, *Pyrrhus et Cin*éas, p. 105.
[377] Simone de Beauvoir, *The Ethics of Ambiguity*, p. 18.
[378] Simone de Beauvoir *The Prime of Life*, p. 549, p. 550.
[379] Seen in this light, the claim to set oneself through one's own projects as transcendence could also be regarded as a specification required by a certain society and its norms. The request for assuming freedom, existence, would then be only the expression of society's demand that is ele-

had emphasized the importance of society for the realization of projects. If within a society suppression is abound then everyone or at least certain people are hindered in their development, "the oppressor feeds himself on their transcendence and refuses to extend it by a free recognition."[380] Oppression is then presented in a deceptive way as "a natural situation since, after all, one cannot revolt against nature."[381]

Recognition – Subject – Transcendence: Conceptual and Methodological Foundations of *The Second Sex*

Beauvoir started working on the *Second Sex* in October 1946 and had completed it by June 1949. During this time she had undertaken a four-month trip to the USA, which left a lasting impression on her. She was confronted with racism, but also with the fact that woman, even though she often displayed the spirit of revenge, still remains a dependent and relative being: "America is a masculine world,"[382] she concludes in her memoirs and her travel journal *America Day by Day*.

The end of World War II met with drastic changes: the victory on the part of the allies made way in Europe for establishing the right to vote for women in France, the UN proclaimed equal rights for women and segregation in the

---

vated to a certain historical momentum. In fact, Beauvoir mentions in *The Second Sex*, that "it is male activity that in creating values has made of existence itself a value." Simone de Beauvoir, *The Second Sex*, p. 65.
[380] Simone de Beauvoir, *The Ethics of Ambiguity*, p. 83.
[381] Ibidem, p. 83.
[382] Simone de Beauvoir, *Force of Circumstance*, p. 133.

USA was officially banned. Beauvoir was influenced by these changes to a considerable extent: "I began to realize how much I had gone wrong before the war, on so many points, by sticking to abstractions. I now knew that it did make a very great difference whether one was Jew or Aryan; but it had not yet dawned on me that such a thing as a specifically feminine 'condition' existed."[383] However, this had sparked her interest, and even though she had encountered very different women, they had all shared the same experience – "they had lived as 'dependent persons'".[384]

This, however, had not sufficed to inspire her to write a book about women. It was rather conceived by chance at the time when she actually wanted to write a book about herself. In the course of her conversations with Sartre, she was confronted with the fact that the first question should actually be: "What had it meant to me to be a woman? At first I thought I could dispose of that pretty quickly. I had never had any feeling of inferiority, no one had ever said to me: 'You think that way because you're a woman'; my femininity had never been irksome to me in any way. 'For me' I said to Sartre, 'you might almost say it just has not counted.' 'All the same, you weren't brought up in the same way as a boy would have been; you should look into it further.' I looked, and it was a revelation: this world was a masculine world, my childhood had been nourished by myths forged by men, and I had not reacted to them in at all the same way I should have done if I had been a boy."[385] From this point on, Beauvoir's interest in this topic was to

---

[383] Simone de Beauvoir, *The Prime of Life*, p. 572.
[384] Ibidem, p. 572.
[385] Simone de Beauvoir *Force of Circumstances*, p. 103.

be deep and long-lasting. She gave up on the idea of writing about herself and decided instead to approach the situation of woman in general. In contrast to her writings which were inspired by her personal experiences, at the age of forty, Beauvoir discovers by chance a central aspect of her personality: being female. For Beauvoir, gender relations had been of no interest up until 1945. Far from suffering from her femininity, she writes in her memoirs, she had on the contrary, from the age of twenty onwards enjoyed the advantages of both sexes.[386] It was because of this privileged position, she emphasizes, it had been possible for her to write *The Second Sex*.[387]

The Social Dimension of Transcendence

In *The Second Sex* Beauvoir voices a fundamental criticism directed towards patriarchal society that reserves transcendence and freedom only for men. In summary, her main thesis is the following: women are excluded from recognition as a subject, they are turned into the Other and pushed into the sphere of immanence. Beauvoir gives a social aspect to the idea of transcendence: it represents the public sphere dominated by men where the subject can achieve recognition through productive work, through the realization of deliberately chosen projects as well as through creating values, whereas the female part represents the sphere of immanence characterized by repetition, sustainment and continuity, and furthermore involves the

---

[386] Ibidem, p. 199.
[387] Ibidem. p. 199.

sphere of life and privacy and does not spare any room for the realization of individual projects.[388]

Already in *The Ethics of Ambiguity* Beauvoir had developed the first approaches towards a social dimension of the notion of transcendence by equating life-sustaining activities not with transcendence but rather with immanence, and thus referring indirectly to the situation of women. "Life is occupied in both perpetuating itself and in surpassing itself; if all it does is maintain itself, then living is only not dying, and human existence is indistinguishable from an absurd vegetation; a life justifies itself only if its effort to perpetuate itself is integrated into its surpassing and if this surpassing has no other limits than those which the subject assigns himself."[389] Oppression divides the world into two clans: those who enlighten mankind by thrusting it ahead of itself and those who are condemned to mark time hopelessly in order merely to support the collectivity. Those people's lives are restricted to the sheer repetition of mechanical gestures; their leisure only allows for gathering new energy; the oppressor devours their transcendence and refuses to continue it through free recognition. In order to combat insurgency, oppression is presented deceptively as naturally given.[390]

---

[388] See also: Eva Lundgren-Gothlin, *Simone de Beauvoir's ‚The Second Sex'*, p. 242. Eva Lundgren-Gothlin points out the fact that Beauvoir developed a concept of transcendence that deviates from that of Sartre, it is oriented towards Hegel and Marx .In Sartre's work, the intentional act and the project are not oriented towards social categories and thus housework is to be also regarded as a project.

[389] Simone de Beauvoir, *The Ethics of Ambiguity*, p. 82, 83.
[390] Ibidem, p. 83.

In *The Second Sex,* Beauvoir refers to Hegel who made the concept of recognition a central philosophical category and developed an ontology of the sexes, classifying men and women into two different social spheres. She shows how the woman is excluded from the public sphere, from accessing the world and from transcendence. The woman remains rooted in the state of necessity, in life and immanence. Thus she is not able to participate in the struggle for recognition which is part of the important process of becoming a subject. On the other hand Beauvoir relies on the potential for change addressed in Hegel's dialectics. Hegel introduced "becoming" and thus the process of change into "being". Therefore the fact that women are nowadays inferior in relation to men could be transformed into the question "should that state of affairs continue?"[391] For: "the verb *to be* must be rightly understood here; it is in bad faith to give it a static value when it really has the dynamic Hegelian sense of 'to have become.'"[392]

According to Beauvoir, the myth of femininity that is constructed around the woman, subsequently creates a timeless image of the woman, leading to her suppression and exclusion due to her pre-assigned natural inferiority, but to criticize this, thus not mean, that we cannot speak about women any more. Beauvoir develops a new concept of recognition consisting of two parallel movements: on the one hand, the request for equality – all human beings are freedom and transcendence – and on the other hand, a request for the recognition of differences[393]. Not to accept

---

[391] Simone de Beauvoir, *The Second Sex*, p. XXX.
[392] Ibidem, p. XXX.
[393] As demonstrated by Herta Nagl-Docekal the theme of equality and

such concepts as the eternal feminine, she points out, is not to deny that women exist today, this denial is no liberation for those concerned, but rather a flight from reality.[394]

Beauvoir's main interest focuses now on how it was possible that a struggle for recognition had never occurred between man and woman or respectively that the woman "has never stood forth as subject before the other members of the group."[395] This question, however, cannot be understood without further explanation of the concept of the subject, upon which Beauvoir bases her theories.

The Concept of the Subject

Whereas Beauvoir does not attempt in any way to define the concept of recognition in more detail, she approaches the problem of the subject again and again and at length. She is utilizing different concepts of the subject without, however, differentiating between them more explicitly. Nonetheless, a thorough explanation would be necessary in order to demonstrate that the problem of recognition can be found in different spheres, concerning the different ways of

---

recognition of differences still plays a central part in feminist political philosophy. She emphasizes that the request for recognition does not necessarily have to coincide with the rejection of the equality posit. Herta Nagl-Docekal, *Gleichbehandlung und Anerkennung von Differenz: Kontroversielle Themen feministischer politischer Philosophie*, in: *Politische Theorie. Differenz und Lebensqualität*, Hg. von Herta Nagl-Docekal und Herlinde Pauer-Studer, Frankfurt/M.: Suhrkamp 1996, p. 9–54.
[394] Simone de Beauvoir, *The Second Sex*, p. xx.
[395] Ibidem, p. 698.

existing and acting in which the subject is involved. Thus, a distinction shall be made between

1. the subject of existence
2. the subject of morality
3. the subject of dominance.

However, the distinction between different concepts of the subject does not imply that they exist in their pure forms. Furthermore, it does not imply that man/woman contain a plurality of subjects within themselves, but that he/she "is" a subject that unifies different claims and dimensions, that can be differentiated philosophically-hermeneutically. Even though Beauvoir apparently utilizes the subject of dominance as such in certain parts, we must consider that this subject of dominance also poses a certain claim for morality. In the same way the subject of existence can repeatedly claim dominance. The subject of morality itself is not neutral in respect to dominance, it can either question dominance or claim it exclusively for itself.

The Subject of Existence

For the existentialist every subject is primarily an existing one, transcending the given situation. "An existent", as Beauvoir emphasizes in *The Second Sex* "*is* nothing other than what he does; the possible does not extend beyond the real, essence does not precede existence: in pure subjectivity, the human being *is not anything*. He is to be measured by his acts."[396] One cannot give an answer to the question what a woman is. According to Beauvoir, one can say whether a peasant woman is a good or bad worker, whether an actress is talented or not "but if one considers a woman in her immanent presence, her inward self, one can say absolutely nothing about her, she falls short of having any qualifications."[397] In response to the question of *"what she is"*,[398] no answer can be found. This is not due to the fact that the hidden truth was too vacillating for it to be encircled, but because there is no truth in this matter: in "human society nothing is natural and (...) woman, like much else, is a product elaborated by civilization."[399] In an interview with Margaret Simons dating back to 1985, Beauvoir emphasized that she had always agreed with Sartre in this respect and had adopted his theory: "I have never believed – nor Sartre either, and on this point I am his disciple – we never believed in human nature".[400] Understanding what the rejection of human nature within existentialism means is of utmost importance for the interpretation of *The Second Sex*.

"If man as the existentialist sees him is not definable", writes Sartre "it is because to begin with he is nothing. He will not be anything until later, and then he will be what he makes of himself. Thus, there is no human nature, because there is no God to have a conception of it."[401] Sartre's and

---

[396] Simone de Beauvoir, *The Second Sex*, p. 257.
[397] Ibidem, p. 257.
[398] Ibidem, p. 257.
[399] Ibidem, p. 725.
[400] Margaret Simons, *Beauvoir Interview (1985)* in: *Beauvoir and the Second Sex*, p. 134.
[401] Jean-Paul Sartre, *Existentialism and Humanism*, London: Methuen 1973, p. 28.

Beauvoir's existentialism assumes an atheist position in contrast to the philosophical-theological tradition that assumes the existence of a God as a creator. When we think of God as a creator, we are thinking of him, most of the time, as a supernal artisan. Whatever doctrine we may be considering, whether it be a doctrine like that of Descartes or Leibniz, we always imply that the will follows more or less from reason or at least accompanies it, so that when God creates he knows precisely what he is creating. "Thus the conception of man in the mind of God is comparable to that of the paper-knife in the mind of the artisan: God makes man according to a procedure and a conception, exactly as the artisan manufactures a paper-knife, following a definition and a formula."[402] In the philosophical atheism of the eighteenth century, the notion of God is suppressed, but not, for all that, the idea that essence is prior to existence. Be it Diderot, Voltaire or even Kant: man possesses a human nature, which means that each man is a particular example of an universal conception, the conception of Man, and this essence of man precedes that historical existence which we confront in experience.

Sartre concludes that if God does not exist, there is at least one being whose existence is before its essence: "Man is nothing else but that which he makes of himself."[403] Existentialism radicalizes the concepts of modernity by detaching existence, subject and freedom from the concept of the human being, and by regarding it as a flexible ontological fundamental structure of each existing human individ-

---

[402] Ibidem, p. 27.
[403] Ibidem, p. 28.

ual.[404] Furthermore, this involves a deconstruction of any rule of reason or nature which had formed in place of a Godly rule in the 18th century. In *Pyrrhus et Cinéas,* Beauvoir points out that there does not exist a natural order, "according to which one's position would be defined by the position of all others. (...) In order to occupy a given place in the world, the individual himself would have to be a given: a pure passivity. He would never, therefore, question the end result of his actions: He would not act. "[405]

As the human being is free however, he cannot *have* a certain place on earth. He rather *assumes* his place by throwing himself into the world, thereby causing his own existence through his project in the midst of other humans. No pre-assigned order determines the world anymore nor the place that a given human being assumes in it: "He does not feel at all like a cog in a given machine, on the contrary, he feels that there is no part of the world that is meant for him: he feels like a spare part".[406]

The existence of the human being is not justified by any means or even necessary from the beginning onward, a fact that Beauvoir painstakingly points out in all her works. Rather the human being has to justify his existence through

---

[404] Sartre points out in *Being and Nothingness* that we shall find little help in Kantians. In fact, they preoccupied themselves with establishing the universal laws of subjectivity which are the same for all, and never dealt with the question of *persons*. Moreover, for them the subject was only the common nature of those persons. Jean-Paul Sartre, *Being and Nothingness*, p. 225.
Beauvoir emphasizes repeatedly that Hegel denies individuality, that only the spirit is considered as a subject: "but *who* is a subject?" she writes in *The Ethics of Ambiguity*, p. 105.
[405] Simone de Beauvoir, *Pyrrhus et Cinéas*, p. 46.
[406] Ibidem, p. 46.

his deeds in the first place, to give his existence a reason to found himself. Beauvoir addresses this unmistakably in *The Second Sex*: "Every individual concerned to justify his existence feels that his existence involves an undefined need to transcend himself, to engage in freely chosen projects".[407] Only through my deeds do I justify my existence, not through the fact that I simply live: "There is no justification for present existence other than its expansion into an indefinitely open future."[408] Bourgeois society however is aiming at attributing to the woman, due to her sex and her nature, a certain place in society from birth on. Thus, she is assigned – opposite to man – a place within a "natural order" which she does not have to fight for, but that is pre-assigned to her from birth. To be restricted to a certain place and a certain activity due to nature presents for Beauvoir however – as she is attempting to demonstrate throughout her entire work – an intolerable form of suppression and exclusion. This suppression and exclusion means that the human being is transformed into an object, into a thing. The woman would be pre-assigned to certain characteristics and abilities from the beginning without having the possibility to question the goals of her acts, moreover she would not be able to act at all.

The Subject of Morality

The fact that one has no pre-assigned place in the world opens up many possibilities that would not otherwise be

---

[407] Simone de Beauvoir, *The Second Sex*, p. XXXV.
[408] Ibidem, p. XXXV.

given if our place was already fixed by society. Yet it also involves a permanent tension, a permanent struggle in order to conquer one's place in the world and to defend it thereafter. Furthermore, the future has to be open, enabling the realization of new projects. However, this openness is threatened from two different angles: a relapse can occur at any time from transcendence into immanence whenever the subject gives up its freedom by choice and escapes from it or because the relapse is imposed on him. Thus, an additional moral dimension is necessary that on the one hand turns towards the subject of existence with the request to become aware of its moral dimension on the other hand rejecting the claim for dominance by others who claim transcendence only for themselves. Beauvoir exceeds here Sartre's ontological concept of freedom and develops the notion of 'moral freedom' in terms of one's own deliberate decision "to will to be free". The idea is to escape the temptation to escape one's own freedom and to put up resistance against all demands for domination by others who claim freedom only for themselves. The subject of existence is always in a area of tension between the subject of morality and the subject of dominance. In *The Second Sex* Beauvoir points out that the subject of dominance claims its being-a-subject only for itself and excludes all the others by denying, in order to maintain its dominance, that freedom is already innate of every subject inasmuch as it is already transcendence. The subject of dominance sets itself up as the essential, in order to constitute the Other as the inessential, the object.[409] Beauvoir points out that this subject of domi-

---

[409] Simone de Beauvoir, *The Second Sex*, p. XXiii.

nance has always been a male one: "He is the Subject, he is the Absolute – she is the Other."[410]

The subject of dominance is connected to the subject of morality in two ways: on the one hand it needs morality and uses it for legitimizing itself as the absolute subject and on the other hand it requires being the only one to decide about morality: good and evil, as well as just and unjust. Beauvoir demonstrates how morality was used by the discourse of the ruling forces as a mechanism for exclusion being turned against women.

The Subject of Dominance

Beauvoir supposes in *The Second Sex* that the subject of dominance is just as old as humanity itself and that the category of the Other is just as original as consciousness itself.[411] In primitive societies, in the oldest mythologies there is a duality between the equal and the Other, that however at first was not characterized by gender separation. Otherness is moreover a "fundamental category of human thought".[412] The feminine element at first was no more involved in such pairs as "Sun-Moon, Day-Night" than it was in the contrasts between Good and Evil, Right and Left, God and Lucifer.[413] Beauvoir refers to Lévi-Strauss who had pointed out, that the passage from the state of Nature to the state of Culture is marked by man's ability

---

[410] Ibidem, p. xxii.
[411] Ibidem, xxii.
[412] Ibidem, p. xxiii.
[413] Ibidem, p. xxiii.

to view biological relations as a series of contrasts:"duality, alternation, opposition, and symmetry, whether under definite or vague forms, constitute not so much phenomena to be explained as fundamental and immediately given data of social reality."[414] These phenomena, however, would be incomprehensible if in fact human society were simply a *Mitsein* based on solidarity and friendship. Things become clear on the contrary, if, following Hegel, we find in consciousness itself a fundamental hostility toward every other consciousness: "the subject can be posed only in being opposed – he sets himself up as the essential, as opposed to the Other, the inessential, the object."[415]

According to Beauvoir, in order to become a subject, a voluntary positioning is necessary – an act of self-positioning. The subject has to differentiate himself/ herself from solidarity and friendship based on *Mitsein* through an act of opposition. Male and female live together within a primordial *Mitsein*. The bond, however, that unites the woman to man is not comparable to any other. The woman has never broken this original *Mitsein*. That is one of the reasons why the man was able to constitute the woman as the Other: she did not raise the claim for being a subject because she considered her relation to the man as necessary without, however, reciprocating it.[416] The couple is, according to Beauvoir, a fundamental unity with its two halves riveted together which makes the cleavage of society along the line of sex impossible.

---

[414] Ibidem, p. xxiii.
[415] Ibidem, p. xxiii.
[416] Ibidem, p. xxv.

Beauvoir uses the term *Mitsein* in a contradictory way. While in certain parts it signifies friendship and solidarity, here it expresses a state where the subject has not yet formed itself. In *The Second Sex*, Beauvoir mentions that the woman was often worshipped as the Other, but only in order to constitute her alterity as absolute and irreducible and in order to exclude her from *Mitsein*. In this way *Mitsein* is depicted as something that women are not only born into due to a biological fact but also as something that can be denied to them. On the one hand *Mitsein* stands for friendship and solidarity, a dimension of human-reality that is not characterized by "fundamental animosity" as seen by Hegel. *Mitsein* based on friendship and solidarity focuses on the possibility of a mutual recognition where the freedom of the one enables that of the Other. This concept of *Mitsein* poses an alternative to the concept of the subject that constitutes itself by a hostile act of opposition.

Does then Beauoir also suppose two different types of consciousness? A consciousness that generally assumes a hostile position against any other consciousness, and one that does not have this general hostility? Do they exist simultaneously and how do they relate to one another? How does a subject develop out of *Mitsein*? One thing can be concluded from what has been said before: the subject constitutes himself/herself by differentiating himself/herself from an "initial *Mitsein*" after having set himself/herself in hostile opposition to Others.

Beauvoir demonstrates how a collective subject could be constituted: villages, tribes, nations and classes gain their unity through opposing other villages, tribes and nations or classes. Through positing themselves as common subject they gain unity through setting boundaries and through affiliating with Others. Thus, the subject is seen as a collectivity that forms its identity through a general attitude of hostility towards the Other, wanting to dominate the Other. As a matter of fact, however, wars, festivals, trading, treaties, and contests among tribes, nations, and classes tend to deprive the concept of the Other of its absolute sense and to make manifest its relativity; "willy-nilly, individuals and groups are forced to realize the reciprocity of their relations."[417]

Let us now raise some questions related to this: under which conditions would a single member of a village, a tribe or a kingdom, dare to oppose the leader of the tribe or the king, in order to posit himself as an individual subject? Under which conditions would the members of a household – the woman, the sons, the daughters for example – begin to set themselves as individual subjects opposite the Pater Familias? Beauvoir mentions nothing about the hierarchies that exist within a collective subject, whether the women are completely excluded from any power or not and which place they take in the whole hierarchy.

However, when we look back in history we learn about considerable changes taking place after the Middle Ages: Dominance was no longer legitimated by God but needed a specific legitimation. After the French Revolution the dominance of one single individual, the king for example, was questioned and along with the request for equality and freedom of all humans began the quest for new ways of social organization and legitimation. From this moment on the issue of recognition becomes important.

---

[417] Ibidem, p. xxiii.

The Concept of Recognition

When considered from a philosophical perspective, the concept of recognition has been introduced relatively recently. In *Multiculturalism and 'The Politics of Recognition'* Charles Taylor brings up the thesis that a connection exists between recognition and identity.[418] Identity as self-understanding of the human being, as consciousness of certain characteristics which make them human, depends at least partly upon recognition or non-recognition. Non-recognition or misinterpretation can cause suffering, some sort of repression and can leave his victims behind with tormenting self-hatred and painful wounds. Recognition is therefore a human basic need.

The philosophical concept of recognition originates in Hegel's work and its reference can be traced back to Fichte. Hegel's early works characterize the process of recognition still in an individual, intersubjective way, whereas this perspective is abandoned later increasingly in favor of a philosophy of the spirit. While Hegel's objective in his earlier works is to reconstruct the process of the formation of a universal consciousness through the struggle for recognition based on the actions and interactions of individual consciousnesses, in the *Phenomenology of Spirit* he concentrates on the experience and the manifestation of the spirit.[419]

---

[418] Charles Taylor, *Multiculturalism and 'The Politics of Recognition'*, Princeton: Princeton University Press 1992.

[419] This is the reason why Axel Honneth goes back to Hegel's earlier works, elaborating the thesis that social conflicts arise from the violation of moral claims leading to struggles for recognition. Axel Honneth, *Kampf um Anerkennung, Frankfurt am Main: Suhrkamp 1994.*

When dealing with the problem of the existence of the Other, Sartre refers in *Being and Nothingness* explicitly to Hegel's master-slave chapter in the *Phenomenology of Spirit*.[420] According to Sartre, "Hegel's brilliant intuition is to make me depend on the Other *in my being*. I am, he said, a being for-itself only through another."[421] Due to the fact that I must necessarily be an object for myself only over there in the Other, I must obtain from the Other the *recognition* of my being.[422] Thus, for Sartre, immense progress had been made: first of all, negation which constitutes the Other would be direct, inner and mutual and furthermore a negation that touches every consciousness deep within its being: "I find that being-for-others appears as a necessary condition for my being-for-myself".[423] However, Sartre also considers Hegel to be guilty of an epistemological optimism in assuming that through the authority of the Other's recognition of me and my recognition of the Other, an objective agreement is realized between the consciousnesses "I know that the Other knows me as himself".[424] But there is no common measure between the object-other and the I-subject. Furthermore, Hegel is also guilty of a more fundamental form of optimism, namely an ontological one, for in his eyes truth is the truth of the whole. Hegel himself assumes the perspective of truth, that is of the whole, in order to approach the problem of the Other: he does not put

---

[420] A.V. Miller translates Hegel's chapter "Herrschaft und Knechtschaft" with "Lordship and Bondage". G.W.F. Hegel, *Phenomenology of Spirit*, Oxford: Oxford University Press 1977, p. 111-118.
[421] Jean-Paul Sartre, *Being and Nothingness*, see above, p. 237.
[422] Ibidem, p. 237.
[423] Ibidem, p. 238.
[424] Ibidem, p. 240.

himself into an individual consciousness but moreover he forgets his own consciousness: he *is* the whole.[425]

The Master-Slave Dialectics in *The Second Sex*

In *The Second Sex* the Hegelian master-slave dialectics plays a pivotal role concerning the topic of recognition and the exclusion of women. Beauvoir writes that according to Hegel, the privilege of the master takes form when he risks his life in the struggle for recognition in order to gain and when he overcomes his fear of death and the spirit prevails over life. However, the one who surrenders, not having risked his life enough to succeed, emerges from this struggle as a slave. Nevertheless he had faced the same risk and therefore a sort of reciprocity can be seen between master and slave: in this struggle always being led by men, slaves are also granted a certain equality. "Whereas woman is basically an existent who gives life and does not risk *her* life; between her and the male there has been no combat".[426] For women had never entered this form of reciprocity, they became the absolute Other. Therefore, Beauvoir differentiates between the 'Other' and the 'absolute Other' where the latter can never acquire any sort of reciprocity. The misfortune on the part of the woman lies in the fact that she "is biologically destined for the repetition of Life"[427], whereas the modern women today rightfully demand "to be recognized as existents by the same right as men and not to sub-

---

[425] Ibidem, p.243.
[426] Simone de Beauvoir, *The Second Sex*, p. 64.
[427] Ibidem, p. 64.

ordinate existence to life, the human being to its animality."[428] Furthermore, Beauvoir writes in her historical overview in *The Second Sex* that the human race has always sought to escape its specific destiny. The support of life became for man an activity and a project through the invention of the tool, "but in maternity woman remained closely bound to her body, like an animal."[429] She maintains the life of the tribe by giving children their daily bread. "She remained doomed to immanence."[430] The woman was not creative in any field in contrast to the man who changed the world through his deeds, who transcended the given and brought forth the new: "He made conquest of foreign booty and bestowed it on the tribe; war, hunting, and fishing represented an expansion of existence, its projection toward the world. The male remained alone the incarnation of transcendence."[431] The man gradually transformed his experience into action and the male principle triumphed in his imagination and his practical existence: "Spirit has prevailed over Life, transcendence over immanence, technique over magic, and reason over superstition".[432] The devaluation of woman represents – according to Beauvoir – a necessary stage in the history of humanity due to the fact that the woman based her prestige not on her own positive value but on the weakness of the man: "In woman are incarnated the disturbing mysteries of nature, and man escapes her hold when he frees himself from nature".[433] In his work

---

[428] Ibidem. p. 65.
[429] Ibidem, p. 65.
[430] Ibidem, p. 73.
[431] Ibidem, p. 73.
[432] Ibidem, p. 75.
[433] Ibidem, p. 75.

he stands his ground against nature as a sovereign will and reinvents the world. At the same time he increases his access to the world. In this activity he puts his power to the test; he sets up goals and opened up roads toward them; "in brief; he found self-realization as an existent".[434] His only aim is not to sustain the world but to disrupt its limitations. Those nations though, Beauvoir surmises that are still under the influence of the mother gods and that have adhered to a matrilineal system remained at a primitive stage of civilization. Only after the man had started to dethrone the woman was he able to realize himself and to recognize the male principle of creative force, of light, of intelligence and of order.[435]

Beauvoir assumes that every society leans toward a patriarchal mode after man had acquired clearer self-consciousness, "once he dares to assert himself and offer resistance".[436] Even beforehand when still worshipping the magical powers of the woman, when he was still perplexed about the mysteries of Life, of Nature, and of Woman, he was never without his power. When, terrified by the dangerous magic of woman, he sets her up as the essential, it is he who poses her as such and thus he who really acts as the essential in this voluntary alienation. "In spite of the fecund powers that pervade her, man remains woman's master as he is the master of the fertile earth; she is fated to be subjected, owned, exploited like the Nature whose magical fertility she embodies"[437].

---

[434] Ibidem, p. 63.
[435] Ibidem, p. 76.
[436] Ibidem, p. 73.
[437] Ibidem, p. 73.

The triumph of the patriarchate had neither been a matter of chance nor the result of violent revolution. "From Humanity's beginnings, their biological advantage has enabled the males to affirm their status as sole and sovereign subjects."[438]

Here, Beauvoir expresses the tension between humanity and the woman: humanity is not just a natural species that strives for sustaining its kind but wants to transcend itself. In setting himself up as the subject, man posits the woman as the Other, whereas the woman is placed as the Other by the man. "For the male it is always another male who is the fellow being, the other who is also the same, with whom reciprocal relations are established".[439]

Beauvoir points out, that we have to distinguish between two forms of alterity or Otherness.[440] One form of alterity – the category of the *Other* – is as basic as consciousness itself. A duality can be found in the most primitive societies and the oldest mythologies: "that of the Self and the Other."[441] The other form of alterity is the category of the absolute Other: "To be the absolute Other" Beauvoir points out means to be "without reciprocity."[442] To the degree at which woman is regarded as the absolute Other – that is to say, whatever her magic powers, as the inessential – it is impossible to consider her as another subject.[443] Because woman was made into the absolute Other she was excluded from the status of the subject. The woman, concludes

---

[438] Ibidem, p. 77.
[439] Ibidem. P. 70.
[440] Ibidem, p. 71.
[441] Ibidem, p. xxii.
[442] Ibidem, p. 141.
[443] Ibidem, p. 71.

Beauvoir, was not recognized by the man as equal because, for biological reasons, she remained subjected to reproduction. This in turn let her not participate in the struggle for recognition out of the initial *Mitsein* in order to place herself as a subject. She never shared man's way of working and thinking, because she remained in bondage to life's mysterious processes. The male did not recognize in her a being like himself. "What was unfortunate for her was that while not becoming a fellow work-man with the laborer, she was also excluded from the human *Mitsein*."[444]

Here Beauvoir argues again in a contradictory manner: whereas on the one hand *Mitsein* comprises the part of life from which the woman had failed to differentiate herself, namely the familial part, the area of reproduction, on the other hand Beauvoir considers *Mitsein* as the area of active work, the area of production where the master-slave dialectics gains importance. The slave is able to achieve recognition through work, for the master-slave-dialects have according to Beauvoir "its source in the reciprocity that exists between free beings".[445] A man can challenge and combat the sovereignty of the Other at any time. That is the reason why the master is always worried that the slave could rebel against him and challenge his dominance.

Even as a slave the man preserves his initial freedom that makes him challenge and combat the sovereignty of his master. The woman on the other hand does not represent any danger to the man because she does not challenge his sovereignty, nor does she combat it. Whereas the other man, even as a slave, is considered as equal inasmuch as he

---

[444] Ibidem, p. 77.
[445] Ibidem, p. 141.

is freedom and transcendence, the woman does not dispose of this initial freedom. We are here confronted with a problem that has already been discussed in connection with *The Ethics of Ambiguity*. Beauvoir regards the human being as an ambiguous existence, as freedom and necessity, transcendence and facticity, being-in-itself and being-for-itself. In *The Second Sex,* Beauvoir makes a further step: man remains transcendence and being-for-itself even as a slave and from this position he is able to question the dominance of the master and fight against him. The woman however, represents the absolute Other, that is denied from any form of equality and reciprocity. In this case the woman is reduced to a passive victim, a relative being that had been set by men and that is dependent on them and only existing through them.

Beauvoir, however, had always resisted to see the woman solely as a victim. In her work, we are therefore apparently confronted with two contradicting lines of argumentation. One showing that the woman was set as the absolute Other by the man and thus condemned to immanence. That is the reason for her being unable to participate in the struggle for recognition and therefore never accomplishing the status of a subject. But without the participation in the struggle for recognition, no independent existence as a subject can take place. The condition for participation is defined according to gender: while slaves are able to participate, women are excluded from participation due to their biological determination. When adhering to this argumentation, the process of recognition represents the necessary prerequisite for being a subject. Every exclusion therefore means remaining in the state of being-in-itself, of immanence, and to be unable to realize being a subject, being-for-itself and freedom. In this approach the environment, the corresponding situation, the Other and the general conditions in society play a decisive role: they determine whether I am a subject or whether I am able to become one. Therefore, I am dependent upon factors that I cannot control. Beauvoir, however, also attempts another direction in her argumentation: every human being is an autonomous freedom, regardless of his or her situation. Every human being is transcendence and freedom from the beginning of his/her life. The woman discovers and chooses herself as an autonomous subject even if men force her to adopt the role of the Other. What particularly signals the situation of woman, Beauvoir points out in the introduction to *The Second Sex*, is "that she – a free and autonomous being like all human creatures – nevertheless finds herself living in a world where men compel her to assume the status of the Other."[446] Thus, it looks as if Beauvoir would develop two different models of recognition. On one side, the model of recognition serves the purpose of bringing forth subjects and on the other side, already constituted subjects and autonomous freedoms come together.

Yet Beauvoir does not make this distinction. Her interpretation of the Hegelian master-slave dialectics and the focus on work as a relevant aspect of liberation is strongly determined by Marxist ideas. Both Beauvoir and Sartre turned toward and tackled Marxism after World War II. Additionally it shall be noted that the Hegelian master-slave dialectics would never have assumed such a central position in the history of ideas as it later did without Karl Marx. Beauvoir's master-slave dialectics have to be inter-

---

[446] Ibidem, p. xxxv.

preted therefore by taking the Marxist thesis of liberation through work into account without however, losing track of Beauvoir's individual approach to Hegel.[447]

Besides this, exclusion from work is not the only reason for transforming the woman into the absolute Other, rather the worst curse that was laid upon woman, was "that she should be excluded from these warlike forays. For it is not in giving life but in risking life that man is raised above the animal; that is why superiority has been accorded in humanity not to the sex that brings forth but to that which kills."[448]

Recognition is therefore only given to those that overcome life and do not fear death. The master risks his life in such a way that he prefers death to surrender, while the slave is not ready to risk his life and prefers a life in servitude as opposed to death. Femininity however is confronted

---

[447] There is no doubt that a whole generation of left-orientated French intellectuals was influenced by Hyppolite's and Kojève's interpretations of Hegel. The thesis of Eva Lundgren-Gothlin that "the influence of Hegel evident in *The Second Sex* is mediated via the French tradition of Hegelisanims, and particularly by the interpretation of Kojève" seems to me to be problematic. Eva Lundgren-Gothlin, *Sex and Existence. Simone de Beauvoir's the Second Sex*, London: Wesleyan University Press 1996, p. 67.
Beauvoir was very sceptical about all concepts of salvation – either through history or through Spirit. Beauvoir reports in her memoirs that she had a discussion with Queneau about the 'end of history': Queneau, who had been initiated into Hegelianism by Kojève, thought that one day all individuals would be reconciled in the triumphant unit of Spirit. 'But what if I have a pain in my foot?' I said. '*We* shall have a pain in your foot,' Queneau replied. While, as we can see, Beauvoir refers here explicitly to Queneau, she never refers to Kojève in any of her works. Simone de Beauvoir *Force of Circumstances*, p. 43.
[448] Simone de Beauvoir, *The Second Sex*, p. 64.

with the inverse problem: it does not celebrate death as overcoming life but gives life by overcoming death. The woman risks her life every time she gives birth; and despite that she is excluded from the entitled recognition – at least in a model of war ethics as espoused by Hegel. She gives life, she does not take it. Far from receiving recognition for the production of new life this is rather, at least in a society that considers overcoming life as being of higher importance than life itself, the starting point for female suppression. In a patriarchal society the exclusion of the woman is based on her biological ability to give life. The power and recognition that she deserves due to her ability to give life is taken from her in the patriarchate: she is reduced to an instrument of reproduction, to an object. She is under the dominance of the man who seizes control over the female body. However, it was to take several years after the first publication of *The Second Sex* for Beauvoir to regard herself as a radical feminist and fight for birth control and abortion.

Due to the fact that the woman does not engage in a hostile confrontation with the man she represents, according to Beauvoir, the embodiment of a male dream: "She is the wished-for-intermediary between nature, the stranger to man".[449] She opposes him with neither the hostile silence of nature nor the hard requirement of a reciprocal relation. Thanks to her, there is a means for escaping that implacable dialectics of master and slave which has its source in the reciprocity that exists between free beings.[450] This is the tragedy of the "unfortunate human consciousness": each

---

[449] Ibidem, p. 140.
[450] Ibidem, p. 141.

separate conscious being aspires to set himself up alone as sovereign subject. Each tries to fulfill himself by reducing the other to slavery. But the slave, through his works and fears, senses himself somehow as the essential and by a dialectical inversion, it is the master who seems to be the inessential.[451] In the case of the woman, however, man hopes to be able to escape these relentless dialectics by setting the woman as the absolute Other. "Woman thus seems to be the inessential, who never goes back to being the essential, to be the absolute Other, without reciprocity".[452]

Yvanka B. Raynova shows very clearly that Beauvoir supplements Sartre's initial project of the human being, i.e. to want to make himself into God, with a gender specific aspect: Sartre's initial project does not include everyone but only men. In the case of the women, we encounter the complementary initial project of being-for-others It was Sartre's merit to point out that the fundamental project of being-for-itself, namely a in-itself-for-itself, that is God and thus grounding for itself, to want to become its being, is doomed to fail. Yet it was Beauvoir who brought the initial project of women into the open, namely the female project of being-for-men.[453] This project – according to Beauvoir – is however, just as inauthentic: "Woman is pursuing a

---

[451] Ibidem, p. 140.
[452] Ibidem, p. 141.
[453] Yvanka B. Raynova, *Das andere Geschlecht im postmodernen Kontext*, in: *L'Homme. Zeitschrift für feministische Geschichtswissenschaft*, 10. Jg. Heft 1, Wien: Böhlau 1999, p. 89. See also: *Le deuxième sexe: Une lecture postmoderne*. In: *Le deuxième sexe: Une relecture en trois temps, 1949-1971-1999*, sous la direction de Cécile Coderre et Marie-Blanche Tahon, Montréal : les éditions du remue-ménage, 2001, p. 141.

dream of submission, man a dream of identification."[454] Beauvoir emphasizes that women, in never having set themselves as a subject, have never created any religion or literature of their own: "Woman do not set themselves up as Subject and hence have erected no virile myth in which their projects are reflected: they have no religion or poetry of their own: they still dream through the dreams of men. Gods made by males are the gods they worship".[455] The Woman sees herself and makes her choices not in accordance with her true nature in itself, "but as man defines her".[456]

The Myth of Femininity

Beauvoir explores in *The Second Sex* the role of male ideas and myths regarding women which form the basis for her exclusion as a sort of simulacra. In order to gain better understanding of the nature of the myth, Beauvoir proposes to take a look at what it was used for.[457] For it is difficult to describe a myth; "it cannot be grasped or encompassed; it haunts the human consciousness without ever appearing before it in fixed form".[458] For example, women can be seen as: idol, slave, source of life and power of darkness, the elemental silence of truth and deceitfulness, chatter and lie; healer and witch; prey of the man and his downfalls. This comes from not regarding woman positively, such as she herself considers herself to be, but negatively, such as

---

[454] Simone de Beauvoir, *The Second Sex*, p. 719.
[455] Ibidem, p. 142.
[456] Ibidem, p. 137.
[457] Ibidem, p. 260.
[458] Ibidem, p. 143.

she appears to man.[459] Beauvoir points out that the myth of woman, sublimating an immutable aspect of the human condition – namely, the "division" of humanity into two classes of individuals – is a static myth. "It projects into the realm of Platonic ideas a reality that is directly experienced or is conceptualized on a basis of experience; in place of fact, value, significance, knowledge, empirical law, it substitutes a transcendental Idea, timeless, unchangeable, necessary.[460] The myth is a transcendent idea that escapes the mental grasp entirely. Thus, as against the dispersed, contingent, and multiple existences of actual woman, mythical thought opposes "the eternal feminine, unique and changeless."[461] If the definition provided for this concept is contradicted by the behavior of women in flesh and blood, it is the latter who are wrong: we are told not that femininity is a false entity, but that the women concerned are not feminine. The contrary facts of experience are impotent against myth. "To pose Woman is to pose the absolute Other, without reciprocity, denying against all experience that she is a subject, a fellow human being."[462]

Beauvoir demonstrates that only few myths have proven to be of such advantage for the ruling caste as that of the woman: it justifies all privileges and even authorizes their abuse.[463] The woman is necessary for the joy of the man and his triumph to the point where it could be said that if she had not already existed, men would have invented her.

---

[459] Ibidem, p. 143.
[460] Ibidem, p. 253.
[461] Ibidem, p. 253.
[462] Ibidem, p. 253.
[463] Ibidem, p. 255.

And indeed, Beauvoir writes: "They did invent her".[464] The representation of the world, like the world itself, is the work of men; they describe it from their own point of view, which they confuse with absolute truth. "Thus humanity is male"[465] Beauvoir follows, and man defines woman not in herself but as relative to him; she is not regarded as an autonomous being. Her determination and differentiation is based on the relation to man, whereas his is not in reference to her. "She is the incidental, the inessential as opposed to the essential. He is the Subject, he is the Absolute, she is the Other".[466]

Men wanted to sustain their male predominance. That is the reason they had invented the separation in society between immanence and transcendence: "Men have presumed to create a feminine domain – the kingdom of life, of immanence – only in order to lock up women therein."[467] The man likes to make reference here to Hegel who legitimized these two separate areas through his philosophy: "With other men he has relations in which values are involved; he is a free agent confronting other free agents under laws fully recognized by all; but with woman – she was invented for the purpose – he casts off his responsibility of existence, he abandons himself to the mirage of his *en-soi*, or fixed, lower nature, he puts himself on the plane of inauthenticity."[468] The woman on the other hand does not only believe that truth is something *other* than what men claim it to be. She recognizes, rather, that there is not *any* fixed

---

[464] Ibidem, p. 186.
[465] Ibidem, p. xxii.
[466] Ibidem, p. xxii.
[467] Ibidem, p. 65.
[468] Ibidem, p. 613.

truth.[469] Not only the becoming of life, not only the magical phenomena that surround her and undermine the idea of causality prompt her suspicion against the principle of identity: in the midst of the male world that she herself belongs to, she perceives in herself the ambiguity that is innate in every principle, each value, everything that exists. She is aware of the fact that male morality is a deception in respect to the woman. Art, literature and philosophy all represent attempts "to found the world anew on a human liberty: that of the individual creator; to entertain such a pretension, one must first unequivocally assume the status of a being who has liberty."[470] The ability to set oneself as autonomous freedom was however explicitly denied to women. In order to enable the woman to become a creator herself, all the restrictions that have been imposed on women would have to be eliminated.

Beauvoir notes here that Hegel's philosophy produces the exclusion of women. However much Hegel's philosophy implies a potential for emancipation and change, it creates the areas of immanence and transcendence in the first place thus enabling the legitimization of the dominance of man over woman. The areas of family-immanence and public-transcendence are not complementary in Hegel's work but rather, as has already been shown, outlined in a hierarchical way. The status of the subject can be attained only through participation in public life, that is in transcendence.

Beauvoir demonstrates that Hegel's philosophy implies an irresolvable contradiction in respect to gender relations.

---

[469] Ibidem, p. 612.
[470] Ibidem, p. 711.

On the one hand, Hegel's philosophy could be seen as the philosophy of freedom par excellence, as its aim is the gradual realization of freedom and transcendence in the world and not merely a shifting of transcendence into an afterlife. On the other hand however, women are excluded from access to transcendence because of their nature. They are kept in immanence including the entire areas of reproduction, education, care and interpersonal relations that make a society viable in the first place. If women, for example, would break out of these areas and leave them behind in order to set themselves as subjects in the area of transcendence, this would inevitably cause a lot of troubles. Thus, the myth of woman is utilized for imprisoning women in the private sphere. This implies several benefits: firstly, the provision of the vital area of reproduction is secured, secondly, it enables the exclusion of women from recognition and competition. In this conception that is not based on complementarities nor on mutuality, immanence represents a hierarchically lower level that is to be transcended and that is equated with femininity. Thus it is not surprising that all activities connected to this area not only have no value but that femininity itself is regarded as something that is without any value and that needs to be transcended. Only to take part in the struggle for recognition will enable women to attain the status of a subject. If one is to adhere to this conception then femininity has to be given up, in order to be able to become a subject.

Even though Beauvoir is aware of the pitfalls within the Hegelian system, she partly follows the same misogynous tendency in *The Second Sex* by equating the nature of the woman, her biological determination, as well as the activities connected to reproduction, with immanence, in order to depreciate them and to contrast them to transcendence. Consequently, such activities are not considered as projects. Here Beauvoir adheres to the nature-culture-problem encountered in modernity: modernity judges humans on what they do. Modernity assumes a depreciative position toward all processes that occur by nature, without creation by humans, as nature is as a stage that requires transgression and dominance by the human being.

Beauvoir assumes that the myth of woman can emerge only in those cultures that have attained a certain level of prosperity: "The myth of woman is a luxury. It can appear only if man escapes from the urgent demands of his needs."[471] According to Beauvoir the fellah of ancient Egypt, the peasant Bedouin, the medieval artisan and the contemporary worker has in the requirements of work and poverty relations with his particular woman companion which are too definite for her to be embellished with an aura either auspicious or inauspicious.[472] Here Beauvoir addresses an issue that is essential for the understanding of *The Second Sex*: that is the limitation of the thesis of the woman as the absolute Other from a regional and historical perspective as well as from a sociopolitical perspective. The woman was not excluded at all times and in all nations from the active *Mitsein,* from work. Amongst the medieval artisans, work still took place within the domestic area where the woman still played an essential economic role. Also, in the case of the fellah in ancient Egypt, the women were responsible for the economic provision of the household. Beauvoir furthermore points out that the myth of

---

[471] Ibidem, p. 260.

[472] Ibidem, p. 260.

woman did not find its adequate place in the working classes: it was poverty that forced women to work and prevented them to be turned into the absolute Other.

Mutual Recognition: Friendship

In *The Second Sex* Beauvoir seeks a way out of the endless struggle for recognition, she looks for "a means for escaping that implacable dialectic of master and slave".[473] Beauvoir attempts to find a possibility to encounter another subject as a subject, without necessarily having to oppose it from the start. She sees this possibility in friendship. In friendship it is possible to rise above this conflict "if each individual freely recognizes the Other",[474] each regarding himself and the Other simultaneously as object and as subject in a reciprocal manner.

It is striking that Beauvoir considers this reciprocity realized specifically in the case of lesbian women: "in exact reciprocity each is at once subject and object, sovereign and slave".[475] However, it is not the refusal of wanting to make oneself into an object that leads the way for women into homosexuality. Most lesbians rather try to cultivate the treasures of their femininity. A man would be able to reveal the existence of her flesh *for herself,* not however for what it represents *to others.* "It is only when her fingers trace the body of a woman whose fingers in turn trace her body that

---

[473] Ibidem, p. 141.
[474] Ibidem, p. 140.
[475] Ibidem, p. 416.

the miracle of the mirror is accomplished".[476] Caressing is not a means for appropriating the partner but rather to gradually find oneself through her. The possibility exists to try out different roles and to follow new paths where both partners can remain autonomous subjects. In spite of her appreciation of female homosexuality Beauvoir does not draw any conclusions for a political strategy. Beauvoir thus in her theory does not elaborate further on the concept of female homosexuality as an expression for mutual recognition.

The concept of friendship is only mentioned briefly by Beauvoir in order to make way for the master-slave dialectics thereafter. For friendship, she points out, is not an easy virtue. It is moreover the highest achievement of the human being that paves his way to the truth. "But this true nature is that of a struggle unceasingly begun, unceasingly abolished, it requires man to outdo himself at every moment."[477] This authentic moral attitude, however, can only be achieved by the human being "when he renounces *mere being* to assume his position as an existent".[478] Through this transformation he/she also renounces all possessions, for possession is one way of seeking mere being. It is the existence of other men/women that tears each man/woman out of his/her immanence and enables him/her to fulfill the truth of his/her being, to complete himself/herself though transcendence, through escape toward some objective, through enterprise.

Even if not completely elaborated on, a new concept of the subject is proposed by Beauvoir in a few short lines: the

---

[476] Ibidem, p. 416.
[477] Ibidem, p. 140.
[478] Ibidem, p. 140.

subject does not set himself/herself by opposing and proving his/her only authority against the Other, moreover the subject is formed only through the existence of another human being, who enables him/her to live his/her transcendence and his/her project. Without the help of other people, without the recognition through others, I may remain helplessly in the state of immanence. Only the encounter with other humans who support me, open up to me the joys of transcendence and offer me the possibilities for realizing my projects, who actually open my eyes to the fact that I am able to create my own projects; only this makes it possible for me to fulfill myself as transcendence. The freedom of the other that confirms my freedom can in turn be confirmed in his/her freedom as well, however this does not have to necessarily happen. Another possibility would be to arrive at a conflicting situation with one another. Inasmuch as the subject actually sets himself/herself through his/her projects as transcendence, conflicts can arise. However this is not imperative, moreover a project could also be enabled through the Other in the first place. Friendship, therefore, is according to Beauvoir "a true alterity."[479] I recognize that there exists a consciousness separate from mine and substantially identical to mine.

Thus we can differentiate between three types of alterity in Beauvoir's work:

1. Alterity as the absolute Other: this conception determines Beauvoir's thesis of the woman as the absolute Other. It is the man who is the subject positing the woman as the absolute Other, without her being able to reverse this position.

---

[479] Ibidem, p. 140.

2. Alterity as the constituting characteristic of identity: the subject is only able to set himself/herself by opposing an existing Other and attempts to dominate this Other that stakes the same claim. In the struggle for recognition, a common level is now sought where the Otherness can be transformed in favor of sameness, for Otherness basically represents danger. This concept determines Beauvoir's master-slave-dialectics;

3. Alterity as the condition for friendship where each individual freely recognizes the Other, each regarding himself/herself and the Other simultaneously as object and as subject in a reciprocal manner, without seeking to dominate the Other.

Here, Beauvoir attempts in a few lines to contrast the absolute claim of the subject of dominance with a new subject relation, namely that of friendship. While the subject of dominance requires the Other for limiting and negating it in order to be able to set himself/herself as a subject, in friendship I recognize that the Other has a consciousness as well, which is coequal with mine, that he or she is also freedom and transcendence and thus I do not try to set myself as the only sovereign consciousness. It is not attempted to abolish this alterity, but rather the real, concrete alterity is the prerequisite for real friendship.

Beauvoir introduces here a concept of alterity and mutual recognition that unfortunately she fails to develop any further. Therefore many questions remain unanswered. When she says in reference to Hegel that in every consciousness a fundamental hostility against any other consciousness can be found and it stakes the claim to set itself as the only sovereign subject, how is then such an alterity possible? How can it develop? Is the only possible way to become a subject to be involved in the struggle for recognition? Is this a necessary condition for a moral attitude? Does humanity have to transgress this process in order to be ready for true friendship? Does this imply for women that they have to enter the struggle for recognition, or is another way possible as well?

As we can see, Beauvoir does not reserve as much room for positive solutions as she does for conflicts. This is not only found in the case of friendship but also in that of recognition in general. However, the key to all positive solutions can be found in the problem of the subject, that will be now addressed concretely in respect to the woman as a subject.

The Woman as Subject

As we have seen in detail, Beauvoir's main thesis in *The Second Sex* is that the woman is constituted by a male subject as the absolute Other. Beauvoir however departs from this thesis by attempting to develop a way out of this negative determination: the woman must be seen in a positive way "such as she seems to herself to be."[480] While the first part of *The Second Sex* is dedicated to facts and myths that made it possible to turn the woman into the absolute Other, in the second part, Beauvoir attempts to find a way for the liberation of the woman in the context to lived experience. The concrete experience of women shall be taken seriously. Beauvoir emphasizes that the modern woman is about to

---

[480] Ibidem, p. 143.

override the myth of woman: she starts claiming her independence in a concrete way.

The objective of the following is to point out whether Beauvoir succeeds in developing an image of the liberated woman, furthermore, to illustrate which solutions she proposes and in which dilemmas she entraps herself along the way.

Beauvoir poses the question of the woman on several different levels. As we have seen she starts with the subject: just like any other human being the woman represents an autonomous freedom, a subject. However, she is confronted with a situation "in which she is the inessential".[481] The drama of the woman consists in the conflict between her being a subject and the requirements of a situation that constitutes her as an object. The woman is – just like Africans, Jews and all those that are excluded and discriminated – made into an object, into a thing, by assigning a certain identity to her that cannot be changed: someone is a woman or a black person, for having special fixed characteristics, just as a table or chair that are unchangeably what they are. The situation is equated to the identity and is presented as unchangeable. For this purpose the body plays an important role: it is said that you are a woman due to your female body having certain characteristics and performing certain tasks and functions.

The question about the woman arises therefore on three levels that are interconnected, although this is not explicitly addressed by Beauvoir: on the level of the situation, on the level of the body and on the level of identity. However, the distinction of these three levels does not imply that they exist in their pure forms nor that the woman consists of

---

[481] Ibidem, p. xxxv.

these three levels, but that these levels comprise different problems that can be differentiated hermeneutically. In order to comprehend the woman as a whole these three levels have to be considered jointly. This leads to the question, how they are actually connected and what importance they have in connection with the question about the woman. All three levels "coexist" on the primary level of existence: each human existence takes place in a concrete situation and it is equipped with a body and must "create" its own identity.

However, Beauvoir does not differentiate in such an explicit manner. In order to gain a better understanding of the problems that are encountered on the way of liberating the woman, she attempts to carefully analyze the traditional destiny of the woman. This is the reason why she gives a voice to the woman in her second book of *The Second Sex* as *lived experience*. Here Beauvoir makes a distinction between the formative years and the situation. The chapter *The Formative Years* includes the subchapters: *Childhood, The Young Girl* and *the Lesbian,* whereas the woman is only addressed in the section entitled *Situation*. The latter is sub-divided further into the following sections: *The Married woman, The Mother, The Prostitute* and *From Maturity to Old Age*. The part entitled *The Formative Years* at the beginning of the second book is introduced with Beauvoir's most famous quotation: "One is not born, but rather becomes, a woman".[482] Subsequently, this sentence led to extensive speculation from her readers. Here it shall be shown that Beauvoir intended to say one thing in particular: a person is not born as a woman but as a child. While

---

[482] Ibidem, p. 267.

Beauvoir repeatedly emphasizes the fact that being a woman represents a situation that reflects a cultural condition and thus is not a natural one, childhood represents for her a "natural" situation. According to Beauvoir the situation of the woman only starts with her marriage, whereas in the case of childhood and of lesbians she does not refer to the woman, but rather to the future woman. For instance she sees hardly any difference in the development of the child up to the age of twelve between both sexes: "In so far as he exists in and for himself, the child would hardly be able to think of himself as sexually differentiated."[483] Even if the girl appears to be gender specified long before the onset of puberty, sometimes even during early childhood, then this is not the case due to secret instincts urging her to immediate passivity, to coquetry, to motherhood, but due to the fact that from birth onwards others interfere in the life of the child and because her vocation is forced into her during the first years of her life. Beauvoir points out, that only if others mediate can an individual become the *Other*. The girl is conditioned from an early age to refrain from the realization of free projects and to instead retreat to certain activities and spaces. The interference in her fate by others exists from birth and it would lead to an entirely different result if guided in a different way. She is not only deprived of her transcendence and her freedom: she is made from early childhood on by a general consensus into a woman.

Beauvoir refers back to the structure previously developed in *The Ethics of Ambiguity* where she differentiates two situations, namely a "natural" one, that is the situation of childhood, one that the woman is forced into, and then

---

[483] Ibidem, p. 267.

one where one is able to and has to choose, which is determined by a "moral decision" of wanting to be free. The first part of our book has approached this ethical dimension of transcendence and the problem of childhood as a developmental process in detail. Childhood is one of the reasons for Beauvoir why man attempts to escape his freedom: "The misfortune which comes to man as a result of the fact that he was a child is that his freedom was first concealed from him and that all his life he will be nostalgic for the time when he did not know its exigencies."[484] The situation of the woman approaches that of the child: the child is in need of fixed and pre-assigned values for the purpose of orientation. However – as Beauvoir adds in *The Ethics of Ambiguity* – there are also humans, such as former slaves or women in certain cultures that live in a childlike world throughout their entire life: "They can only submit to the laws, the gods, the customs and the truths created by the males."[485] Thus, a collective process of awareness is necessary as well as an individual one for adapting moral freedom: what is needed is an individual and collective conversion. The decision for freedom that reveals itself to the child on the threshold of adolescence is neither predictable nor determined, just as the collective liberation of a society can neither be determined nor irreversible.

Beauvoir argues here on different levels. Her requests are located on the individual level just as much as on the level of society. Only the demystification of the myths surrounding the female nature, the "eternal feminine" and the transition to free self-determination, and accepting one's

---

[484] Simone de Beauvoir, *The Ethics of Ambiguity*, p. 40.
[485] Ibidem, p. 37.

own responsibility in authenticity, can enable us to pave the way for the creation of a new situation where women are recognized as subjects, as equal in being, transcendence and freedom. Then it will be possible for individual women, too, to follow this way toward self-realization.

In connection with the above, two lines of argumentation can be distinguished in Beauvoir's work:

1. *The request for deconstruction:* Society develops myths that produce a certain image of the woman: she is made to be the absolute Other, beyond any reciprocity, determined by concepts that are not her own. This limits the woman to certain activities, she is deprived of all possibilities of realizing her projects, she is furthermore deprived of her transcendence and her being a subject. This leads therefore to a manipulation of her being a subject: her being a subject is questioned. Only when the woman is no longer determined in a negative manner by the man and by a social situation, only when the myth of the woman is deconstructed that renounces her being a subject, will the woman be able to set herself in a positive way, just as she wants to be "for herself".

2. *The request for emancipation:* Women have to be released from the dominance of the man. The woman is subject, transcendence and freedom, just as man. Humanity can only be realized through both genders. For this purpose, a new democratic society is needed where there is no longer place for the absolute Other and nobody is made into an object or idol any more. A society is requested that allows for an open future to all humans, including women, and for the setting of new goals and of new opportunities. The measure for this is the possibility to realize an individual project. Only a society that enables the individual, in-

cluding the woman, to realize his or her projects makes it possible that "the eternal feminine in the totality of her economic, social, and historical conditioning"[486] is finally annulled. The attempts of individual women to realize transcendence within immanence do not suffice for changing the situation of suppression. Hence, a universal change of society and a collective liberation is needed.

The Question of Woman

"Are there women, really?"[487] This is the question which introduces the series of questions attempting to find a definition for what a woman is. Because it would appear "that every female human being is not necessarily a woman; to be considered as such she must share in that mysterious and threatened reality known as femininity. Is this attribute something secreted by the ovaries? Or is it a Platonic essence, a product of the philosophic imagination?"[488] Beauvoir describes how, since antiquity, satirists and moralists have enjoyed creating a picture of female weakness. Throughout time men have declared satisfaction in being the pinnacle of creation. In this sense, Thomas Aquinas defined the woman, in reference to Aristotle, as a "misbegotten male," who, in comparison, is a deficient, flawed creature. Beauvoir asks whether it is possible that perhaps among humans, women are simply those that are arbitrarily called "woman," as the nominalists claim. But she dis-

---

[486] Simone de Beauvoir, *The Second Sex*, p. 597.
[487] Ibidem, p. xix.
[488] Ibidem, p. xix.

agrees with the followers of the Enlightenment, of rationalism, and nominalism; "woman, to them, are merely the human beings arbitrarily designated by the word *woman*."[489] To Beauvoir, it is impossible that the word 'woman' has no content. She claims that nominalism is a doctrine that falls short and and makes it easy for adversaries of feminism to prove "that women *are* not men."[490] One needs merely to walk through the world with open eyes to see that humanity splits itself into two categories of individuals, whose clothing, faces, bodies, smiles, gaits, interests and activities are obviously different. "Perhaps", Beauvoir states, "these differences are superficial, perhaps they are distinct or disappear. What is certain is that right now they do most obviously exist."[491] To say that woman, like man, is human, would be too abstract. "The fact is, that every concrete human being is always a singular, separate individual. To decline to accept such notions as the eternal feminine, the black soul, the Jewish character, is not to deny that Jews, Negroes, women exist today".[492] The myths construed by society to legitimize the oppression and exclusion of women, Jews and blacks, must be exposed and abolished. To deny that women, Jews, or blacks exist would not mean liberation for those affected, but rather an escape into the inauthentic. No woman could claim, without being untruthful, to be beyond her sex.

Being a woman, however does not represent an unchangeable reality, but rather a becoming. In this process

---

[489] Ibidem, p. xx.
[490] Ibidem, p. xx.
[491] Ibidem, p. xxi.
[492] Ibidem, p. xx.

the woman must be juxtaposed to man, this means one must look at her *possibilities*. Beauvoir points out, that it is only in a human perspective that we can compare the female and the male of the human species: "As Merleau-Ponty very justly put it, man is not a natural species: he is a historical idea."[493] What gives rise to much of the debate is the tendency to reduce her to what she has been, to what she is today, in raising the question of her capabilities; for the fact is that capabilities are clearly manifested only when they have been realized, "but the fact is also that when we have to do with a being whose nature is transcendent action, we can never close the books."[494]

According to Beauvoir, to question what a woman is, does therefore not mean to ask for the unchangeable, timeless being of woman, the "nature" of woman, from which one could then derive the situation of woman. Rather, Beauvoir proceeds from the concrete situation of woman, which she attempts to analyze in *The Second Sex*. If there are women, it is because there exists a "situation of woman", so that to ask about woman means nothing but asking about her condition, the so-called "condition féminine."[495]

---

[493] Ibidem, p. 34.
[494] Ibidem, p. 34.
[495] See : Yvanka Raynova, *Das andere Geschlecht im postmodernen Kontext*, In: *L'Homme. Zeitschrift für Feministische Geschichtswissenschaft*, Wien: Böhlau 199, 10.Jg., Heft 1, p. 80.

Situation

The largest part of *The Second Sex* deals with the analysis of the situation of the woman. Already in the introduction Beauvoir describes the situation as follows: "Now, what peculiarly signalizes the situation of woman is that she – a free and autonomous being like all human creatures – nevertheless finds herself living in a world where men compel her to assume the status of the Other".[496] In the first part of *The Second Sex*, Beauvoir attempts to clarify how the situation of woman has come into existence, "how the concept of the 'truly feminine' has been fashioned – why woman has been defined as the Other – and what have been the consequences from man's point of view."[497] In the second part of *The Second Sex* she describes the situation of the woman from a female perspective. Here the following questions are discussed: How can a human find self-fulfillment within her womanhood? What limits the freedom of woman, and can she overcome these circumstances?

Beauvoir stresses that situations are characterized by the fact that they change and can be changed. A situation, having developed over time, could be dissolved in another time. In this way, it may be that women today *are* generally inferior to men, but it is because their situation allows for fewer possibilities. But the question is whether this state of affairs should remain thus indefinitely. For Beauvoir, to assume that something *is* unchangeably what it *is*, means to give substantial character to the word *"to be"*,

---

[496] Simone de Beauvoir, *The Second Sex*, p. xxxv.
[497] Ibidem, p. xxxv.

when it really has the dynamic Hegelian sense of "to have become."[498]

The term 'situation' in existentialism expresses the innate ambiguity of the human being to be both freedom and facticity simultaneously. There is no freedom without situation. I find myself always in a certain situation, that I did not choose before. Be it in a certain country, a certain environment, in this or that body; I was born into a world that I have not chosen. Without situation there is no freedom. The situation is the starting point, from which I start my projects. Through this, however, the situation is always the already transcended. It is never accessible for me in its pure facticity, because it has always already been transcended towards a certain meaning by my project. One and the same situation therefore is experienced differently by different people; they 'exist' their fatigue, their desire, their joys in differing ways and manners. Everything that man comes across, exists only in so far as he grasps it under the global perspective of his existence. Beauvoir writes that everything gains value only by "the basic project through which the existent seeks transcendence."[499]

However, Beauvoir again and again relativizes her basic existentialist perspective. Although free and condemned to freedom, man hits upon the limits of his freedom and his projects. One of the constraints consists in the fact that not all individual projects are of equal value. Certain projects, namely those that do not claim to leave the private sphere in order to access the world, are allocated to immanence by Beauvoir. There are many women trying to achieve indi-

---

[498] Ibidem, p. xxx.
[499] Ibidem, p. 60.

vidual salvation by solitary effort. "They are attempting to justify their existence in the midst of their immanence – that is, to realize transcendence in immanence."[500] Thus, freedom remains undivided, yet abstract and void. Beauvoir sees the concrete shapes of this abstract freedom in the female archetypes of *The Narcissist*, *The Woman in Love*, and *The Mystic*, to whom she devotes a chapter each. If woman does not have access to the world her freedom remains unfulfilled. "There is only one way to employ her liberty authentically, and that is to project it through positive action into human society."[501] This is why Beauvoir demands deep-reaching collective change, on an economic and social level as well as in the ethical and cultural fields. In any case, one thing is certain for Beauvoir, "that hitherto woman's possibilities have been suppressed and lost to humanity, and that it is high time she be permitted to take her chances in her own interest and in the interest of all."[502]

A further limitation of freedom occurs because there are situations in which the individual is powerless and left without choice. In a certain sense, this view is an expression of an expanded understanding of freedom through addressing the so-called "force des choses", the force of circumstances.[503] Word War II had brought Beauvoir and Sartre to reflect on some basic positions of existentialism. In retrospect, Sartre stated that his main theme in the period of 1943-1960 was his relationship towards Marxism, which he formulated as such: "La vie m'avait appris la force des

---

[500] Ibidem, p. 627.
[501] Ibidem, p. 678.
[502] Ibidem, p. 715.
[503] The title of one of Beauvoir's autobiographies is *Force of Circumstance*.

choses."[504] Already in *The Ethics of Ambiguity*, Beauvoir speaks about the oppressor devouring the transcendence of the oppressed. The lives of these people are limited to pure repetition of mechanical gestures, their periods of leisure are just enough time for them to regain their strength. In *The Second Sex*, Beauvoir points out, "that the evil originates not in the perversity of individuals – and bad faith first appears when each blames the other – it originates rather in a situation against which all individual action is powerless."[505] It does not make sense to blame an individual; the reason for evil is not purely on an individual level. Beauvoir considers the possibility that transcendence falls back to immanence and that a diminution of freedom into facticity can take place. More than Sartre, she stresses an almost Marxist perspective; that certain situations exert such a strong influence that they manage to diminish existence to an "in-itself."

Beauvoir's reflections are complemented by an historical aspect. Her analyses had shown that neither biological nor mental nor economic definitions can construe the shape of the female human being in society. Rather, it was civilization as a whole "that produces this creature, intermediate between male and eunuch, which is described as feminine".[506] The situation of woman is a consequence of an historical process, which has constituted woman as a relative creature and thus has brought about a femininity that is considered as inferior. In addition to the historical process,

---

[504] Jean-Paul Sartre, *Situations IX*, Paris: Gallimard 1972, p. 99. " Life has taught me the force of circumstances."
[505] Ibidem, p. 724.
[506] Ibidem, p. 267.

we also find with Beauvoir an element of developmental psychology. The situation of woman is not only the consequence of an historical process, but must also be revealed with regard to every individual. The entire education of a girl aims at turning her into a woman. Beauvoir shows how a girl is turned into a woman and that this is an irreversible process, because "later on, woman could not be other than what she *was made*."[507]

Thus we find a tension between two different approaches. On the one hand, every human, woman, too, is an autonomous freedom. Whatever the situation may look like, whether men prescribe women to assume the role of the Other or not, it is the woman who discovers and chooses herself in this world. The situation of the woman forms for the woman only the starting point of her choice, yet does not define womanhood as such. From this position therefore, it is possible to design a positive image of womanhood. If all the limitations and obstacles which constrain the possibilities of woman are eliminated, the new woman will be able to define herself as a subject by her projects. On the other hand, however, womanhood and the female situation coincide. Womanhood is defined and brought forward by the situation. This womanhood is predetermined in a thoroughly negative way, as Beauvoir's analysis shows in sufficient detail. No special values or capabilities can therefore be gained from this womanhood, this femininity. From this position it becomes understandable why Beauvoir repeatedly expresses deep mistrust with regard to womanhood, and why she is tempted to orient herself only towards male values.

---

[507] Ibidem, p. 725.

Beauvoir remains ambivalent with regard to these two positions in *The Second Sex*. Even more: she stresses that ambiguity is innate in every principle, every value and in all that exists. *The Second Sex* does allow for a positive image of femininity and searches for possibilities that would have to be offered to women in order for them to discover "the treasures of their femininity," even if it carries misogynic elements in various places, as we have seen.

However, in her later interviews, Beauvoir sees things differently. In an interview from 1972, Alice Schwarzer asks about her vision of a world in which women were liberated. Beauvoir answers that she does not believe that women, if they have attained equal treatment, shall develop something special, special values. It is a fact, that the universal culture, the civilization and the values all have been created by men.[508] Women should rather acquire the values created by men, instead of rejecting them. "What would it mean to reject the male model?" Beauvoir asks: "If a woman learns karate, this is male. And I find it is good that she does it. One must not reject the world of men, because this world is the world in general and our world, too. Women, like men, will create something new. But I do not think that she will create new values. If one believes this, one believes in a female nature, and against this I have been my whole life".[509] In another interview from 1976, she warns of a backlash from what is known as 'feminism of difference'. Although it would be important for women to discover their bodies, one must not "give it a special value. One must not believe that the female body enables a

---

[508] Alice Schwarzer, *Simone de Beauvoir*, p. 57.
[509] Ibidem, p. 58.

new vision of the world."[510] It seems that at least in her later interviews, Beauvoir has given up her ambivalence in favour of a clear rejection of feminine values.

The Body

Beauvoir does not develop explicitly the existentialist concept of the body in *The Second Sex*. Rather, she presupposes the theories of Heidegger, Sartre, and Merleau-Ponty: "If the body is not a *thing*, it is a situation, as viewed in the perspective I am adopting – that of Heidegger, Sartre, and Merleau-Ponty; it is the instrument of our grasp upon the world, a limiting factor for our projects."[511]

As the body is the instrument of our access to the world, the world appears differently depending on the way it is grasped. Woman is weaker than man; she has less muscle strength, fewer red blood cells, smaller breathing capacity; she runs slower, lifts less heavy weights and there is almost no sport in which she could be a match for man: "she cannot stand up to him in a fight."[512] While the proletariat or the blacks can resolve to slaughter the rulers, woman cannot, even in her dreams, extinguish man. According to Beauvoir, the blacks in Haiti, the Indochinese in Indochina and the workers in Russia have united to form an "us" and turned themselves into a subject. They have made revolutions and thus have dissolved a situation that has come into existence over time. Contrary to these, the situation of

---

[510] Ibidem, p. 54.
[511] Simone de Beauvoir, *The Second Sex*, p. 34.
[512] Ibidem, p. 34.

woman is not something that has come into existence through certain developments and events: "proletarians have not always existed, whereas there have always been women. They are women in virtue of their anatomy and physiology".[513] The division of the sexes is, "a biological fact, not an event in human history."[514] The body of woman is one of the essential elements in her situation in the world.[515]

According to Beauvoir woman's access to the world is a limited one; she is less energetic and enduring in the pursuit of projects, and consequently less capable of implementing them. "The woman is adapted to the needs of the egg rather than to her own requirements."[516] Her body is determined by the "species."[517] Starting with menstruation, moving on towards pregnancy and giving birth, woman is faced with a burden "which is of no individual benefit to the woman but on the contrary demanding heavy sacrifices."[518] The subordination of woman under her species leads to deep estrangement. "Woman, like man, *is* her body; but her body is something other than herself."[519] Only after menopause is woman liberated from the constraints of womanhood; she is no longer subject to powers that are beyond her: "she is herself".[520] These biological facts, as Beauvoir explains, are a key to understanding

---

[513] Ibidem, p. xxiv.
[514] Ibidem, p. xxv.
[515] Ibidem, p. 37.
[516] Ibidem, p. 27.
[517] Ibidem, p. 25.
[518] Ibidem, p. 29.
[519] Ibidem, p. 29.
[520] Ibidem, p. 31.

woman, but they do not establish for her a fixed and inevitable destiny.[521]

For Beauvoir, these facts cannot be denied, "but in themselves they have no significance."[522] As soon as one adopts a human perspective and interprets the body on a basis of existence, biology becomes an abstract science. The burden of the reproductive function of woman can no more be theoretically measured than her access to the world. It is not merely as a body, but rather as a body subject to taboos, to laws, that the subject is conscious of himself and attains fulfilment: "it is with reference to certain values that he evaluates himself. And, once again, it is not upon physiology that values can be based; rather, the facts of biology fake on the values that the existent bestows upon them."[523] If respect or fear of woman prohibit the use of force against her, even the overpowering muscular strength of man no longer represents a source of power: "the 'weakness' is revealed as such only in the light of the ends man proposes, the instruments he has available, and the laws he establishes.".[524] Nature represents for him reality only to the extent that it is included in his actions.

Therefore, the body plays a central but contradictory role. It determines the situation of the woman without, however, determining womanhood completely, which Beauvoir mainly sees as an historical and not as a natural situation. Nevertheless, the body is the point of departure not only for the access to our world and the first draft of

---

[521] Ibidem, p. 32.
[522] Ibidem, p. 34.
[523] Ibidem, p. 36.
[524] Ibidem, p. 34.

our projects, but also the starting point of woman's exclusion and discrimination. Because of her nature, because of her body which enables the woman to preserve the species, she is turned into the absolute Other and put into a situation that makes her unessential. Beauvoir's existentialist approach rejects any essentialist determination: like every human, woman is what she makes of herself. The body, according to Beauvoir, must be viewed from the vantage point of existence, not vice-versa. Identity is not something predetermined; nobody except the woman herself has to decide what she makes of herself. Already in *The Ethics of Ambiguity*, Beauvoir points out that womanhood is not a natural situation: the woman, at least the modern woman in the Western world, chooses her situation.

This raises the question at which point and by whom this womanhood is chosen. In the chapter *The Formative Years*, it seems as if womanhood is not yet determined. Beauvoir starts this chapter of *The Sexond Sex* with her most famous sentence: "one is not born, but rather becomes, a woman". Aside from all further possible interpretations, here Beauvoir wants to say that we are not born as a woman, but as a child. She does not explicitly speak about being born as a child, but speaks about the human female which can never be determined by any biological, psychological or economic fate. Must every human female become a woman? Must every woman have a female body?

At the outset of the chapter *The Formative Years*, in the section called *Childhood* and *The Lesbian* Beauvoir does not yet, or not at this point, speak of womanhood, but of "the human female."[525] It seems as if there would exist a

---

[525] Ibidem, p. 267.

female body that is not automatically tied to womanhood. When we have a look at the aged woman, we find the reverse situation. Those women who have stopped menstruating are for Beauvoir "no longer females,"[526] which is why in certain cultures they are called "a third sex."[527] Woman is now delivered from the servitude imposed by her female nature. "She is no longer the prey of overwhelming forces; she is herself, she and her body are one."[528] The physiological autonomy expresses itself through the condition of health, balance and strength, which the woman did not possess before.

On the basis of what has been said, can we conclude that Beauvoir sees sexuality and in particular bisexuality as a necessary attribute to existence? Does this mean that sexual determination and being human are identical and simultaneous? Is the anatomical sex a necessary attribute of the human?

In the chapter on *The Data of Biology* Beauvoir investigates the role of the female body by voicing differing scientific and philosophical positions regarding the question "what is a woman?" She starts with a study of the animal world. The outcome is, "that even the *division* of a species into two sexes is not always clear-cut."[529] Nature itself does not supply an answer, because reproduction happens through different means and ways: through cell splitting, through self-fertilization; there are also differing types of hermaphrodism. According to Beauvoir, in humans, the

---

[526] Ibidem, p. 31.
[527] Ibidem, p. 31.
[528] Ibidem, p. 31.
[529] Ibidem, p. 88.

sexes and their relationship to each other are determined by the fact that they are sexually active: "but sexual activity is not necessarily implied in the nature of the human being."[530] A consciousness without body or an immortal human being are absolutely unthinkable: an immortal or body-less existence would no longer be what we call human, whereas it is possible to imagine a society which procreates through parthenogenesis or is made up of hermaphrodites. Whilst the perpetuation of the species can be seen as ontologically established, according to Beauvoir, the necessary differentiation of gender cannot be deduced from it. Beauvoir confirms Merleau-Ponty's assertion: "Existence, he says, has no casual, fortuitous qualities, no content that does not contribute to the formation of its aspect; it does not admit the notion of sheer fact, for it is only through existence that the facts are manifested."[531] But she rejects his argument that the sexuality of humans is necessarily tied to their existence. The differentiation of the sexes and bisexuality do not represent an ontological characteristic, rather, sexuality, through the means and ways it is lived, retroactively explores the concrete definition of existence. In contrast to Merleau-Ponty, Beauvoir does not see sexuality as a necessary component, as a necessary attribute to being human. The claim of Merleau-Ponty, but also of Sartre, that "Sexuality is coextensive with existence,"[532] could, according to Beauvoir, be understood in two different ways: firstly, that every experience of the existing person has a sexual significance, secondly, that

---

[530] Ibidem, p. 7.
[531] Ibidem, p. 7.
[532] Ibidem, p. 39.

every sexual phenomenon has an existential import. "Furthermore, as soon as the 'sexual' is distinguished from the "genital", the idea of sexuality becomes none too clear."[533] From the necessity of the perpetuation of the species, one must not deduce sexual differentiation. We can imagine that one day we have "a parthenogenetic or hermaphroditic society."[534]

Thus, Beauvoir assumes the possibility of a society that does not differentiate by sexes. According to Beauvoir, as a result of new reproduction technologies it is conceivable that society would not discriminate by sex, because it would not be necessary for procreation nor for the survival of humanity. Society would then not need to cling to heterosexuality and the couple-formation of man-woman to guarantee reproduction.

Furthermore, it is conceivable that the body itself could also undergo changes. Though natural conditions seem to resist any change, in reality, nature is, like historical reality, changeable. "In truth, however, the nature of things is no more immutably given, once for all, than is historical reality."[535] Bodies are therefore never absolutely established, they too are subject to vicissitude. For example, Beauvoir speaks concretely of the change of the female body and its impact on womanhood. While the childlike female body does not yet represent womanhood, menopause frees woman from her female body and gives an example of a "third sex." The possibility to change one's sex through a

---

[533] Ibidem, p. 39.
[534] Ibidem, p. 7.
[535] Ibidem, p. xxv.

medical operation is not considered by Beauvoir because medical developments were not that advanced at that time.

These, however, are questions that from today's vantage point are gaining more and more importance. *The Second Sex* could in this sense be an significant contribution to the current debate on transsexuality in the feminist movement, which finds itself confronted with the problem of whether men who consider themselves as women, be they operated upon or not, should be accepted into protected 'women areas' and thereby be recognized as women. All of these debates focus around the concept of what it means to be an authentic woman. Thereby, it is shown very clearly that identity ascription has a lot to do with recognition. Some feminist circles reject transgender women, because they were once men. Some do not. Therefore, it is necessary to have certain criteria beyond the biological sex so as to determine whether transgender women should be recognized as having a female identity. The individual choice to feel like a woman and to choose to be a woman seems not sufficient to be accepted in certain feminist circles.

Beauvoir differentiates between self-perception and perception by others, something that could be used in the current discussions about transsexuality. It is not the body-object described by biologists that actually exists, but the body as lived in by the subject. "Woman is female to the extent that she feels herself as such".[536] But where are the limits of the choice? Can I choose to be a man or a woman? How far is my self-perception determined or destroyed by the situation? How far can my individual design surpass the situation? Can I discard my female body and then choose to

---

[536] Ibidem, p. 38.

be male, which is quite possible with the help of modern medicine? Is it sufficient to choose oneself to be a transsexual male/female, to discard the male body/female body, without having an operation? Can I choose being man/woman and still retain my female/male body?

Beauvoir is only marginally interested in these questions. She brings these into play to point out the complexity of the entire line of questioning. The body represents a lived reality only insofar as it is accepted through actions within a society. Sexuality, according to Beauvoir, is not determined by hormones or mysterious instincts, but rather through the ways and means that the body is perceived through its relation to the world, through the foreign consciousness of others. The perception of the body, both my self-perception as well as the perception of the other depends to a large extent on what Sartre calls the "being-for-Others". Beauvoir does not deal further with the problem of self-perception and the perception by others, which is of central importance not only for the understanding of the body, but also for being recognized as a subject. Therefore, a short digression on Jean-Paul Sartre shall bring clarity in this regard.

The body plays a central role in Sartre's philosophy: it influences not only the encounter with the Other, but also forms the pivotal point for an existentialist theory of recognition. In *Being and Nothingness* Sartre differentiates several ontological dimensions of the body: "I exist my body: this is its first dimension of being. My body is utilized and known by the Other: this is its second dimension. But in so far as I am for *others*, the Other is revealed to me as the subject for whom I am an object. (…) I exist therefore for myself as known by the Other – in particular in my very facticity. I exist for myself as a body known by the Other."[537] For Sartre, the problem of the body is therefore directly related to that of the Other.

In the first ontological dimension of the body Sartre pursues the question of how my body is given *for me*, how I feel about my own body. It is therefore about self-perception. First of all it means having a body, that cannot "float" above the world, but rather finds itself in a certain situation. The body is facticity, insofar as one is born without having chosen to. Sartre emphasizes that the situation is not a purely contingent condition: on the contrary, it reveals itself only to the extent to which the for-itself transcends it towards itself. One who suffers from a disability, in continuing to live, takes over that disability, he transcends it towards his projects. He makes it a necessary aspect of his being, and he cannot be crippled without choosing to be so, without choosing the way in which he perceives his disability as unbearable, humiliating, as an object of pride, as the justification for his failures etc. "But this inapprehensible body is precisely the necessity that there be a choice, that I do not exist *all at once*. In this sense my finitude is the condition of my freedom."[538] One's own body is the viewpoint to the world but one cannot have a point of view on one's own body. Therefore, I cannot have a spontaneous and unreflective consciousness of my body, rather one must say that "consciousness exists its body. Thus the relation between the body-as-point-of-view and things is an *objective* relation, and the relation of con-

---

[537] Jean-Paul Sartre, *Being and Nothingness*, p. 351.
[538] Ibidem, p. 328.

sciousnesses to the body is an *existential* relation."[539] The body exists its pain, its lust, its desire. On the reflective level where we are taking our position – i.e., before the intervention of the 'for-others' – the body is not explicitly and thematically given to consciousness.[540] Sartre gives the example of the child: the perception of the child's own body comes chronologically after the perception of the Other.[541] However, and to the extent that I am conscious of existing for the Other, I apprehend my own facticity.[542] "My body as alienated escapes me toward a being-a-tool-among-tools."[543] My body is utilized and known by the Other.[544] With the appearance of the gaze of the Other, my object-being reveals itself to me, meaning my transcendence as the transcended. "It appears to us then that the Other accomplishes for us a function of which we are incapable and which nevertheless is incumbent on us: *to see ourselves as we are*".[545] Sartre considers the body as fundamental for investigating the concrete relationship to Others. Only then could we take up a consistent attitude in opposition to the Other, if the Other were simultaneously revealed to us as subject and object, as transcending-transcendence and as transcended-transcendence, which is basically impossible. So we shall never "place ourselves concretely on a plane of equality, on the plane where the

---

[539] Ibidem, p. 329.
[540] Ibidem, p. 337.
[541] Ibidem, p. 358.
[542] Ibidem, p. 351.
[543] Ibidem, p. 352.
[544] Ibidem, p. 351.
[545] Ibidem, p. 354.

recognition of the Other's freedom would involve the Other's recognition of our freedom"[546]

Identity

To question one's identity is to question 'who' one is. It implies looking at one's particularities and in what way one differs from others, but it also refers to more general questions such as: what is a human being, what does it mean to be an acting human being, a person, a self?[547] The concept of authenticity, which is central to existentialist philosophy, can be viewed in close relation to the concept of identity. Existentialism assumes that one cannot say of another person what he or she 'is'. Identity is not determined, but rather something that is in a constant state of becoming. Only at the end of someone's life can one say who that person was. Therefore it is impossible to write a conclusive autobiography during one's lifetime. In this sense, Beauvoir emphasizes in *The Second Sex* "that when we have to do with a being whose nature is transcendent action, we can never close the books."[548]

The rejection of a fixed identity does not mean however that it is possible to live without an identity, but rather turns against those prerogatives that want to particularly determine a person a priori. Identity is connected in general with the basic structure of the human being as transcendence,

---

[546] Ibidem, p. 408.
[547] Charles Taylor poses this question in a very complex historical context. See: Charles Taylor, *Source of the Self, The Making of the Modern Identity*, Harvard University Press, 1989.
[548] Simone de Beauvoir, *The Second Sex,* p. 34.

and in concrete with the existentialist experience. Identity is determined through action and one's chosen projects. At a later point in time, it may be possible that one chooses to take up a different project, which in turn has an effect on one's identity. Identity then can be lived authentically but also inauthentically, namely, when I flee from my freedom into bad faith. This escape allows me to deny certain relations to the world, to the Other and to myself, which do not suit me. It enables me to close my eyes before the essential ambiguity of human existence. The path towards authenticity or inauthenticity, however, brings another aspect to light. Even if transcendence and freedom constitute the basic determinants of being, a process of awareness is required in order to raise the freedom from the unreflective level to that of reflection. Authenticity demands a reflexive choice, it requires that one becomes conscious of one's freedom but also of the fundamental ambiguity of human existence. This does not only call for an appropriate environment but also for concrete social, political and economic possibilities. Only then will it be possible to transcend the existing towards certain freely chosen projects, and to no longer identify oneself with the given. Only then will it be possible to define oneself via creative projects and thereby give oneself a unique identity.

What does all this mean for womanhood? Who or what is the woman?

Beauvoir emphasizes that there can be no answer to the question *"what* she *is"*[549], but this is not because the hidden truth is too vague to be discerned: "it is because in this domain there is no truth. An existent *is* nothing other than

---

[549] Ibidem, p. 257.

what he does; the possible does not extend beyond the real, essence does not precede existence: in pure subjectivity, the human being *is not anything*. He is to be measured by his act."[550] Here, Beauvoir means that a person can only be judged by his or her projects and not by external characteristics. In this sense one can say of a peasant woman whether she is a good or a poor worker; of an actress whether she has talent or not. However, womanhood in its immanence that is detached of transcendence and the individual projects of a concrete woman evades any quality assessment. Existentialism decidedly rejects all kinds of questions that ask about the nature of the woman, because this would mean to assume a certain essence independent of lived experience.

Can there then be such a thing as a female identity at all? Does there exist an authentic womanhood?

In some parts of *The Second Sex,* Beauvoir develops a positive image of femininity as the authentic form of womanhood. In the chapter on *The Lesbian* Beauvoir speaks of the femininity that is yet to be discovered. She does not see the lesbian as being in the *situation* of a woman, but rather in her *development*, her becoming, in which womanhood is not yet really determined, in which one has not yet been "made" into a woman. Maybe as a result of not having been shaped yet vis-à-vis man by the myth of femininity, the lesbians manage "to cultivate the treasures of their femininity".[551] In other words, femininity is here being referred to as something positive, something valuable that cannot be found within the relationship to a man. "It is only

---

[550] Ibidem, p. 257.
[551] Ibidem, p. 416.

when her fingers trace the body of a woman whose fingers in turn trace her body that the miracle of the mirror is accomplished".[552] While the love between man and woman constitutes an act, love amongst lesbians can be contemplative: "Between women love is contemplative; caresses are intended less to gain possession of the other than gradually to re-create the self through her; separateness is abolished, there is no struggle, no victory, no defeat".[553] Beauvoir assumes a femininity here that can only be recognized and lived out when two women encounter and caress one another. Thus, she speaks of positive femininity in instances when the woman is not reduced to her ordinary womanhood.

Beauvoir sees another aspect of female authenticity in woman's generosity, in which she ceases to think about herself, "she is pure gift, pure offering".[554] Poorly adapted to male society, she is often forced to invent her behavioral forms herself, as she is seldom satisfied with pre-made patterns and clichés. She shows an anxiety that comes closer to authenticity than the showy self-assuredness of the male. This privileged position vis-à-vis men could only be achieved, however, if women reject the deceptions men offer them, which is supposed to be particularly difficult for women of the higher classes of society profiting from the advantages they get from their men. At the end of *The Second Sex* Beauvoir says: only when we "abolish the slavery of half of humanity, together with the whole system of hypocrisy that it implies, then the 'division' of humanity will reveal its genuine significance and the human couple

---

[552] Ibidem, p. 416.
[553] Ibidem, p. 416.
[554] Ibidem, p. 626.

will find its true form".[555] In other words, Beauvoir assumes that if the relationship of dominance between man and woman were to end, there would automatically be space to discover what maleness and womanhood in their authentic form actually mean. Both women and men could then freely develop their individual projects.

All these examples have one thing in common: they emphasize the free project that is not predetermined and restricted by societal conventions and compulsions. One can speak of authenticity, when I can choose myself freely, when I don't satisfy and identify myself with "ready-made forms and clichés".[556] But part of authenticity is also that I face my situation, that I don't close my eyes before it. To be human means being-in-the-world. A free project can only be realized in and through a particular situation. Hence, authenticity demands of the person, of man and woman, that he or she takes up his or her particular situation and transcends it through his or her action.

The question of the identity of the woman, however, just as the question regarding the situation and the body touches only upon the various abstract realms of womanhood. Only the interaction of body and identity on the concrete level of human existence can resolve the question of what it means to exist as a woman.

---

[555] Ibidem, p. 731.
[556] Ibidem, p. 626.

Existence

The complexity of existence consists in the fact that the hitherto discussed separate points of view of the various modes of existence do not exist in the abstract, but rather coexist in a synthetic unity. The body is invariably interwoven with existence: it is located in a synthetic unity that itself can only be understood through the situation, through the relation to the world. The body isn't simply something contingent, something given, it must not be understood as pure facticity, as a necessity, towards which I can act in this or that way based on my freedom. From an existentialist point of view I can never encounter a natural phenomenon as such. The so-called natural phenomena are always already included in my concrete relation to the world. My sleep isn't something that I can, as a natural phenomenon, confront with my freedom. Rather, my tiredness is something that can exist in diverse ways. The various ways in which I can experience my tiredness, as something pleasant, as something to overcome, as a sign of weakness, etc., refer me to my initial project, where my sleep and my relationship towards it are always already co-determined by my being-in-the-world, by my societal realm and its values; aside from the fact that my sleep is accessible to me only through others. Hence the problem consists in understanding the existing person in his or her totality, to think about him or her in his or her existence.

Beauvoir herself continuously emphasizes that her different analyses in *The Second Sex* can only be understood if one takes into account existence as a whole. To question the woman on the level of the situation, on the level of the body and identity, may be helpful, but should not conceal the fact that these are mere abstractions: "The value of muscular strength, of the phallus, of the tool can be defined only in a world of values; it is determined by the basic project through which the existent seeks transcendence".[557] The problem of existence brings us therefore back to our starting point, the project and this in turn leads again to the question of the 'I' or the 'Self.' Who is it, who chooses a particular project?

In the chapter *Freedom and Transcendence* we have was shown that Sartre, unlike Beauvoir, accepts a Self but not an autonomous 'I'. Beauvoir, on the other hand, does not entirely reject the autonomous 'I' and the autonomous will. Even if life has an inexhaustible multiplicity of relationships to the world, it nevertheless "possesses an inner heart, a centre of interiorization, a *me* which asserts that it is always the same throughout the whole course,[558], she writes in her memoirs *All Said and Done*. If, due to Sartre one cannot say what a life 'is', one could nevertheless inquire as to what it forms: "My life has been the fulfillment of a primary design; and at the same time it has been the product and the expression of the world in which it developed. That is why in telling it I have been able to speak of a great deal other than myself".[559]

How is this interplay of self-determination and determination by others, the relationship of individual designs and societal prerogatives to be understood? Where are the limits to my choice? What role does society play in my pro-

---

[557] Ibidem, p. 60.
[558] Simone de Beauvoir, *All Said and Done*, Harmondsworth, New York: Penguin Books 1977, p. 10.
[559] Ibidem, p. 40.

jects and my choice? The analysis of the situation of the woman in *The Second Sex* shows, as we have seen, that the societal influence in 'making oneself' into a woman is very strong. The existentialist thesis of free individual project, of the Making-Oneself-into-Something, is weakened by societal conditioning. Beauvoir consistently reiterates that the attempts of some single women to escape this conditioning are bound to fail. As much as a woman may try, there is no escape from the collective *situation* of the woman, except for a transformation of society by a "social evolution."[560]

From this perspective a certain field of tension arises. On the one hand, the woman, like any human, is an autonomous freedom, who has to choose and to make herself. On the other hand, she finds herself in a situation in which, with or without her consent, she is made into a woman. From this arises the question of decisionmaking: when and who decides to be something, and does an independent decision even exist? Does the woman decide to take on her situation? When does this happen? Is there a child or a girl who decides not to become a woman? But this contradicts the position that Beauvoir developed in the *Ethics of Ambiguity*: The child needs and wants predetermined, fixed values from which it can orient itself, it needs the spirit of seriousness. Therefore, according to Beauvoir, nothing is further from the conception of the child than wanting to choose himself/herself. One cannot expect that the child should stand up against societal values and projects. Is it in the phase of adolescence or later on? Can the woman reject her situation, after she has been made into the Other; does she still have enough power to posit herself as subject? Ul-

---

[560] Simone de Beauvoir, *The Second Sex*, p. 725.

timately everything leads to the question of what relationship exists between individual projects and the societal framework. However, this framework should not be seen to be of equal value, because, as Beauvoir points out, nothing exists outside of a system of human values. At that moment in which the project itself associates with society to a high degree, there is an interdependence between the individual project and its societal determination. In *The Second Sex* Beauvoir shows how the social project of woman becomes a trap, not because womanhood would be a trap *per se*, but because the activities tied to it stand in contradiction to the societal demands of being a subject.

We now see ourselves confronted with the problem, to what extent the situation determines, limits or destroys the choices and projects of a human. The question also arises as to what extent society has already determined my identity before I have the possibility to realize my own individual projects. But Existentialism turns resolutely against determination by the situation. Here Beauvoir does agree with Sartre, even though she stresses the limits of overcoming a situation and therefore the importance of society. Already in the *Ethics of Ambiguity* she demarcates existentialism vis-à-vis Marxism. However, in Marxism, the goal and the meaning of action are defined by human wills; these wills do not appear as free: "They are the reflection of objective conditions by which the situation of class or the people under consideration is defined. (...) Subjectivity is re-absorbed into the objectivity of the given world. Revolt, need, hope, rejection, and desire are only the resultants of external forces. The psychology of behavior endeavors to explain this alchemy."[561] Existential ontology, however, affixes itself in this essential point in opposition to dialectical materialism: "We think" Beauvoir points out, "that the meaning of a situation does not impose itself on the consciousness of a passive subject, that it surges up only by the disclosure which a free subject effects in his project".[562] Although societal influences must not be underestimated, they cannot wholly determine my individual projects and my identity. They can in fact attempt to give me a certain identity, based on my biological original gender or based on the color of my skin. It would be insincere to ignore this. But it would be just as insincere to find oneself content in a forced situation and to deny that it is us who transcend these situations and choose ourselves as what we are. It is in this sense that Beauvoir says: It is clear that no woman can claim to transgress her sex without being in bad faith.[563] She must become aware of her situation and face it. She must recognize that womanhood is tied to the ambiguity of existence, and not to biological gender.

Paths to Liberation

After judicial equity has been achieved Beauvoir considers entering the working world an essential step on the path

---

[561] Simone de Beauvoir, *The Ethics of Ambiguity*, p. 19
[562] Ibidem, p. 20.
[563] This sentence is our translation of: "Il est clair qu'aucune femme ne peut prétendre sans mauvaise foi se situer par-delà son sexe." Simone de Beauvoir, *Le Deuxième Sexe*, Paris, Editions Gallimard 1976, p.13. This very important sentence from the introduction has been omitted in the English translation.

to liberation for woman, a step which provides economic independence. Yet she holds one should not believe that suffrage and work alone would mean complete liberation: today's employment is not freedom, presently most workers are exploited. According to Beauvoir, the myth of femininity is being kept alive in bourgeois society: even though the working woman has become a matter of course, the place and main task of woman is still seen to be within the family. Beauvoir characterizes the situation of the emancipated woman as a conflicting one: it is still required of woman, "that in order to realize her femininity she must make herself object and prey, which is to say that she must renounce her claims as sovereign subject".[564] However the emancipated woman rejects being limited to her female role, to immanence. She does not want to let herself be maimed in her humanity. The area of transcendence that is opened to her through work, however, demands that she renounces her sex, which constitutes a maim equal to being imprisoned in one's sex. Here, Beauvoir points out, that "to renounce her femininity is to renounce a part of her humanity."[565] Yet this does not mean that being human is automatically linked with biological sex. In existentialism a person does not define himself/herself by sex or body. However, one also must not be hindered to choose oneself as man or woman: "through the identification of phallus and transcendence"[566], so Beauvoir, there results that a man is lent male prestige for social and intellectual success. This is why the man is not divided: his destination as human is

---

[564] Simone de Beauvoir, *The Second Sex*, p. 682.
[565] Ibidem, p. 682.
[566] Ibidem, p. 682.

not in contradiction to his destination as man; he does not have to renounce his sex. Yet, according to Beauvoir, the woman must recognize that the choice of herself as autonomous subject comes into conflict with her femininity. "The independent woman – above all the intellectual, who thinks about her situation – will suffer, as a female, from an inferiority complex."[567] So in bourgeois society, woman is faced with an unsolvable problem: her determination as woman contradicts her destination as human. Beauvoir therefore demands a society which enables women the realization of their individual projects. In her critique of bourgeois society she refers to Karl Marx's famous quotation, which assesses the relationship of man and woman as indicative of a society's freedom: "The direct, natural, necessary relation of human creatures is the *relation of man to woman*. The nature of this relation determines to what point man himself is to be considered as a *generic being*, as mankind; the relation of man to woman is the most natural relation of human being to human being. By it is shown, therefore, to what point the *natural* behavior of man has become *human* or to what point the *human* being has become his *natural* being, to what point his *human nature* has become his nature."[568] Beauvoir writes in concluding *The Second Sex*: "The case could not be better stated. It is for man to establish the reign of liberty in the midst of the world of the given."[569]

---

[567] Ibidem, p. 685. Beauvoir herself seems to have suffered from this conflict. See: Karen Vintges, *Philosophy as Passion* and Toril Moi, *Simone de Beauvoir. The Making of an Intellectual Woman*.
[568] Ibidem, p. 731.
[569] Ibidem, p. 732.

At the time of writing *The Second Sex* Beauvoir's hopes lay in the implementation of a socialist world from which she expected an automatic solution of the problems of women. Socialism would assert the equality of all human beings, and refuse now and for the future to permit any human category to be object or idol: "in the authentically democratic society proclaimed by Marx there is no place for the Other."[570] According to Beauvoir it is not too difficult to imagine a world in which men and women are equal, "for that precisely is what the Russian Revolution had *promised*: women raised and trained exactly like men were to work under the same conditions and for the same wages."[571] Marriage would be a free union which both partners could quit at any time. Maternity would also be free, meaning that birth control and abortion would be allowed, and conversely all mothers, single or married, and their children would receive the same undiscriminating rights. Maternity leave was to be paid for by the State, which would also assume charge of the children, signifying not that they would be *taken away* from their parents.[572] In a properly organized society, where children would be largely taken charge of by the community and the mother cared for and helped, maternity would not be wholly incompatible with careers for women.[573] Beauvoir is here indicating that maternity could very well be a project, which does not necessarily have to represent pure immanence. More than that, it depends on society whether a

---

[570] Ibidem, p. 142.
[571] Ibidem, p. 724.
[572] Ibidem, p. 724.
[573] Ibidem, p. 525.

woman, being a mother, can find an open future in which she can concretely realize her projects. Beauvoir notes, that "the close bond between mother and child will be for her a source of dignity or indignity according to the value placed upon the child – which is highly variable – and this very bond, as we have seen, will be recognized or not according to the presumptions of the society concerned."[574] Whether maternity can therefore be a free project depends on the society in which one finds oneself. If woman is no longer subjected to the rule of man and she can freely decide whether she wants a child or not, it would be conceivable to Beauvoir that this area would no longer be counted as immanence, but rather could be seen as a free project. But then all reproductive capacities would have to be newly allocated: men would have to take over functions that were previously allocated and restricted to the female domain.

More than twenty years after *The Second Sex* Beauvoir admits in an interview with Alice Schwarzer that it had been a mistake to believe that the problems of women could be solved alone by turning a society towards socialism.[575] For the socialism that Marx spoke of the socialism that would change mankind never materialized. Only production methods changed. But this change alone does not suffice to change society and humanity. Consequently, so Beauvoir, the traditional roles of men and women remained the same in socialist countries, despite the different economic system. Even in the Soviet Union, women were still exclusively responsible for domestic work and attending to

---

[574] Ibidem, p. 36.
[575] Alice Schwarzer, *Simone de Beauvoir. Rebellin und Wegbereiterin*, Köln: Kiepenheuer & Witsch 1999, p. 44.

children. A lot would still have to be done. One would have to look at the special structure of the family because, according Beauvoir, the modern family is the heritage of the feudal family. Beauvoir incites us to investigate the correlation between patriarchal and capitalist oppression. Class struggle, in any case, she holds is not enough to emancipate women, they must take their fate into their own hands.

In *The Second Sex* Beauvoir points out that the woman must shed her old skin and "cut her own new clothes."[576] Women must face their situation, this means become aware of the mechanism of oppression and exclusion. They should take their own experiences seriously and exchange them with those of other women. Through this it will be shown that particular situations are not merely individual but rather are a contingent of society. Women must become aware that they are an autonomous freedom just like men, and that their situation is only the starting point of their projects and cannot wholly determine their existence. To face a situation, to recognize it and to no longer deny it, already includes a transcendence of the situation: I must decide in which way I want to go on living; I cannot "not" choose myself. First and foremost initializing a process of consciousness brings about a dispute with one's own situation.

Over and over again Beauvoir emphasizes that the woman must discover herself. Woman must, as previously mentioned, discover the treasures of her femininity. The *lived experience* of woman should be taken seriously and become part of the process of liberation. The reflected, conscious decision for femininity as a path to liberation is mentioned in *The Second Sex*, yet is not elaborated upon.

---

[576] Simone de Beauvoir, *The Second Sex*, p. 725.

The conscious choice of femininity could therefore be an important step toward authenticity, without necessarily meaning a relapse into the myth of femininity. It is also in this sense that the end of *The Second Sex* should be understood: "To emancipate woman is to refuse to confine her to the relations she bears to man, not to deny them to her; let her have her independent existence and she will continue none the less to exist for him *also*: mutually recognizing each other as subject, each will yet remain for the other an *other*."[577] Here, Beauvoir is trying to disperse fears that "if man and woman were equal in concrete matters,"[578] the gender difference would be dissolved and there would be no more passion; alternatively, that the emancipation of woman would lead to an assimilation to man. Even if the separation of humans into two categories was no longer made, the miracles of love, desire, and adventure would remain. Yet she leaves open what would constitute the "true shape" of a couple formed by two humans. Only when we abolish the slavery of half of humanity, together with the whole system of hypocrisy that it implies, then the "division" of humanity will reveal its genuine significance and the human couple will find its true form.[579] Only then will the true face of gender difference be revealed, namely whether it is based on a relationship of dominance or whether a free development is possible. To give women the chance to "make themselves" means neither that Beauvoir is clinging to gender difference, which is determined by biological gender traits, nor that gender difference is a nec-

---

[577] Ibidem, p. 731.
[578] Ibidem.
[579] Ibidem.

essary paradigm for Otherness. To leave the Other in his/her Otherness and not to bring it back to identity does not represent a privileged undertaking of a philosophy of gender difference. Rather it expresses the basic principle of existentialism not to surpass the difference as in the Hegelian system but to recognize it as the basis of existence.

In her later interviews Beauvoir rejects a womanhood or *femininity* that is chosen and carries its own values. "I do not believe, that the woman will create new values. If one assumes this, one believes in a human nature – something I have always rejected."[580] However she does not act accordingly toward male values. In the same interview, in which she rejects feminine values, she recognizes the world as a male world and incites women to acquire male values for themselves instead of rejecting them. Although Beauvoir speaks of the eternal feminine as a lie,[581] she speaks nowhere about the myth of masculinity and of the fact that the eternal masculine is also a lie. Beauvoir should, however, following her existentialist approach also expose the assumption of masculine values, of a fixed masculine identity, as a lie. Just as there is no such thing as a predetermined feminine nature, that manifests itself in certain activities, there is no masculine nature that brings out certain values.

The existentialist approach turns against all fixed attributions from outside and demands the recognition of my *own* choice, which is no longer tied to existing attributions. Thus it could very well be possible that I consciously decide to exist beyond my gender. Authenticity in the existen-

---

[580] Alice Schwarzer, *Simone de Beauvoir. Rebellin und Wegbereiterin*, p. 58.
[581] Ibidem, p. 81.

tialist sense means that I take the situation upon myself and transcend it by consciously deciding for my own life: I may be born into a certain culture, be of a certain sex, but this does not mean that I have to identify myself with it; I can choose differently. The existentialist approach promotes a climate of tolerance in which the individual can choose from different options, without being tied to a fixed identity coming from outer traits or attributes. For feminist politics this would mean creating a wide platform of possibilities for the discovery and realization of new feminine life styles, as well as for life forms that exist beyond gender difference. This does not mean granting to women "equality in difference."[582] Beauvoir emphasizes that this egalitarian segregation has resulted only in more discriminations. The problem is not the recognition of a difference but rather the recognition of differences.

New Challenges and *Old Age*

Fifty years after the publication of *The Second Sex*, we can very well say that woman has taken fate into her own hands. To many young women the condition of woman as described by Beauvoir, in which she was made into the absolute Other beyond any reciprocity, seems like a historical description of a past epoch. In most European countries at least one can hardly speak of woman being the absolute Other, being – because of her sex – excluded from the process of recognition and therefore from the process of becoming a subject. We now find a situation of woman

---

[582] Simone de Beauvoir, *The Second Sex*, p. xxix.

where woman to an increased measure is recognized as an autonomous subject and in which she is given the same possibilities as men to realize her individual projects.

If one considers *The Second Sex* only as a philosophical work being interested in the liberation of women, then one could assume, based on the emancipation which took place in the last fifty years, that *The Second Sex* is now only of historical interest. But if we interpret *The Second Sex* not only from the perspective of emancipation, Beauvoir could be seen as the starting point for new investigations which devote themselves to the unsolved questions and challenges of the future.

Reproductive work is allocated to women who increasingly free themselves by having fewer or no children. How will reproduction activities be socially organized in the future? Will the bourgeois family be increasingly replaced by patchwork-families? Women like men now have to fight for recognition and their place in society, even for survival. What role do children play in a world of autonomous, individual projects? How much and from when on are they themselves autonomous beings? What kind of relationship should exist between mother and child? Fewer and fewer women are prepared to enter the unpaid or low paid welfare sector. The questions of the future will therefore focus on who will take over and finance the "care-economy" sector, which does not only include the reproductive work concerning children but also the care for the aged.

Having written *The Sexond Sex* in 1949 Beauvoir did not undertake any further theoretical research on this topic, neither did she renounce any of her assumptions. But twenty years after *The Second Sex* she wrote her second great theoretical work which dealt with the situation of the aged. In her book *Old Age* she applied her concepts from *The Second Sex,* pointing out that the situation of the aged is very similar to the situation of woman: "In masculine myths the woman, the Other, appears as an idol and as a sex-object at one and the same time. Similarly, for other reasons and in another manner, the old man in those societies is both a sub-man and a superman."[583] But there is one big difference: woman is necessary for society whereas old people who lose their power are of no worth to society anymore: they are no longer anything but a burden. They then become, and to a far more radical extent than a woman, a mere object.[584]

Beauvoir is confronted here with a new problem: what should be said about someone who can no longer realize any projects, who is sick and weak, who has problems handling everyday life. "Apart from some exceptions, the old man no longer *does* anything. (...) Time is carrying him towards an end – death – which is not *his* and which is not postulated or laid down by any project."[585] What about all those claims from *The Sexond Sex?* According to Beauvoir there is no justification for our present existence other than its expansion into an indefinitely open future. Every time transcendence falls back into immanence, stagnation, there is a degradation of existence into the *"en-soi"*. Every subject plays his part as such specifically through projects that serve as a mode of transcendence.[586] Following on from this we could ask whether old people still are subjects,

---

[583] Simone de Beauvoir, *Old Age*, Harmondsworth: Penguin Book 1978, p. 97.
[584] Ibidem, p. 100.
[585] Ibidem, p. 244.
[586] Simone de Beauvoir, *The Second Sex*, p. xxxiv.

Beauvoir does not find the answer to this question. Instead she insists in *Old Age* that "men should remain men during the last years of their lives".[587] To guarantee this we need a society that enables old men and women to go on pursuing goals that give their existence a meaning. "One's life has values so long as one attributes value to the life of others, by means of love, friendship, indignation, compassion."[588]

When answering the question of what kind of society would be needed to guarantee that even in his/her last years a human might still be a human, Beauvoir emphasizes that it would be a society in which a human has always been treated as a human. For this there would have to be a total upheaval of the existing society: for it is the exploitation of the workers, the pulveriziation of society, and the utter poverty of a culture confined to the privileged, educated few that leads to this kind of dehumanized old age. The economy is founded upon profit and actually the entire civilization is ruled by profit. Society cares about the individual only in so far as he/she is profitable.

Beauvoir's later work, *Old Age,* is a passionate plea to take responsibility for the weak and old and not to look away when people are exposed to systematic destruction throughout their whole life. The responsibility of each of us as well as of society as a whole is to enable men/women to realize their projects, limited as they may be for old people. From this we can see that projects must not be limited to competitive achievements, but have to comprise every activity that provides meaning and joy. In *The Second Sex,*

---

[587] Simone de Beauvoir, *Old Age*, p. 13. Men in this quotation also include women.
[588] Ibidem, p. 601.

Beauvoir differentiated between projects: those which she associated with transcendence and those which she associated with immanence, like housework. In *The Second Sex* it was her intention to bring women out of their passivity and self-defeat, with the aim that they may posit themselves as subjects and fight for their place in society. From this, her interpretation of being a subject acquired a tone that emphasized their active, competitive and fighting side. *Old Age* adds another quality: not only must the human being not be defined from outside: man/woman is not what he/she 'is', as existentialism states, but to be human means to depend not only on what one is doing or what one is able to do.

Nowadays, in a time when neoliberalism wants to make us believe that everyone is able to make something out of himself/herself by being engaged in competitive projects, women included, this aspect of Beauvoir's *Old Age* adds an additional perspective. In *The Second Sex* we could at points infer that Beauvoir would follow an almost neoliberal line: women have to fight for their place in society and work in order to realize themselves as subjects. But even in *The Second Sex* this claim was always embedded in another one: the claim for a new society, in which work is not exploitation but self-realization. In *Old Age,* the critique of capitalism gains weight: man must not be judged solely by what he/she is doing, but has to be treated as a human being, independently of how much he/she can contribute to society. Long before neoliberalism, Beauvoir describes the powerlessness of people in the face of the capitalist "machine, the crusher of men – of men who let themselves be crushed because it never even occurs to them that they can escape it."[589] More so than in *The Second Sex* she points out the interdependence and dialectics between individual freedom and collective situation. One can only become a human being in a human world. In *The Second Sex* she had pointed out, as did Marx, that from the relation of man to woman one can see to what point a human being has realized his/her *human nature* in his/her concrete everyday life. In *Old Age,* Beauvoir points out that we can also recognize the true character of society in how it deals with those who are no longer able to work.

---

[589] Simone de Beauvoir, *Old Age*, p. 604.

Conclusion

In the course of this study, the extent to which individual passages of *The Second Sex* are in tension or even in contradiction to one another has been illustrated. Thus it becomes clear that on the one hand these tensions stem from Beauvoir's attempt to merge different approaches, but on the other hand they are also tied to the ambiguity of existence itself. In *The Ethics of Ambiguity*, Beauvoir describes the human as an ambiguous being: asserting itself as freedom, as pure internality against which no external power can take hold. Yet at the same time it experiences itself as a thing crushed by the dark weight of other things.[590]

Beauvoir's work can be seen as a pivot between modernity and post-modernity. She attempts to advance the approaches of Kant, Hegel, and Marx from the existentialist perspective. In existentialism, which can be seen as a trailblazer towards post-modernity, the human is not seen as a citizen of two separated, opposing worlds, as for example in Kant's philosophy, but is rather to be seen as existence and ambiguity, which has ontological as well as ethical consequences. Beauvoir's goal is not to surpass the contradictions between freedom and the situation by reconciliation, but rather to think of them as a part of existence. As with humans, life and history are also ambiguous and contradictory. These contradictions cannot be dissolved in an

---

[590] Simone de Beauvoir, *The Ethics of Ambiguity*, p. 7.

alleged harmony, but can only be mastered in a creative way, by sincere engagement in the form of one's own and unique existence.

The Second Sex can be seen as an appeal to authenticity: women should become aware of their specific situation and overcome it through active engagement. The existentialist approach offers a solution that is located beyond an essentialist, but also beyond a constructivistic approach. Naturalistic essentialism assumes an antecedent feminine nature. Idealistic constructivism, however, assumes that everything, even nature, is constructed, be it through societal norms, through language or through discourse. Existentialism goes beyond both of these approaches. On the one hand, it assumes that there is a being which has not been created and founded by us; we are not even the foundation of our own being, thus it turns against idealistic constructivism. On the other hand existentialism points toward the fact that the (female) body cannot be seen as a purely natural fact, from which a (female) nature, a (female) existence would be derived, thus it turns against naturalistic essentialism.

Beauvoir's existentialism, however, makes a conscious decision for femininity possible, to choose femininity as a project, which does not mean that a relapse to essentialization or a return to the myth of woman must take place. This choice is no longer automatically tied to biological gender: just as some men choose femininity as their project, there are biological women that reject any feminine project. A politics of difference which is based on biological attributes would therefore codify individual projects on the basis of certain attributes, without offering chances for new life forms and life designs.

Many questions are still waiting to be examined from the viewpoint of a new epoch, the onset of which was announced in *The Second Sex*. Every era develops its own directions of thought. Just as the philosophies of modernity turned against the feudal prerogatives of ancestry or nobility and therefore readied the path for the bourgeois-capitalist era, so post-modern thinking turns against the legitimization discourse of the bourgeois society, which was built upon oppositions and attempted to dissolve the ambiguity of humanity and the dichotomies of nature and culture, woman and man, and body and spirit, in favor of one direction. This thinking in hierarchical oppositions proves to be unsustainable in an era that is increasingly molded by mass culture, new media and the new technologies. Philosophically and politically, the need for a philosophy of ambiguity becomes apparent, which goes beyond reductionism and thought of opposition. In this regard *The Second Sex* represents a bridge between modernity and post-modernity: in retrospect, it develops a critique of ideologies and gender relationships of modernity, oriented towards the future. It contains visions of feasibility and possibilities that carry with them no other boundary but that of freedom. Yet freedom must not be misunderstood in a neoliberal way, but as the responsibility of each and every one of us, and of society as a whole, to enable all individuals to realize those projects that fill their lives with meaning and joy.

Bibliography

Al-Hibri, Azizah and Simons Margaret A. (eds.). *Hypatia Reborn. Essays in Feminist Philosophy*, Bloomington: Indiana University Press 1990.

Anderson, Thomas C., "Freedom as Supreme Value: The Ethics of Sartre and Simone de Beauvoir", in: *American Catholic Philosophical Association: Proceedings of the Annual Meeting*, 50, 1976, 60-71.

Arp Kristana. "Conceptions of Freedom in Beauvoir's *The Ethics of Ambiguity*", in: *International Studies in Philosophy* 31, no. 2, 1999, 25-34.

Arp, Kristana. *The Bonds of Freedom, Simone de Beauvoir's Existentialist Ethics*. Chicago and La Salle: Open-Court 2001.

Barnes, Hazel. "Self-Encounter in *She Came to Stay*", in: Elizabeth Fallaize (ed.), *Simone de Beauvoir. A Critical Reader*, London/New York: Routledge 1998, 157-170.

Barnes, Hazel. *Response to Margaret Simons*, in: *Philosophy Today,* Vol. 42, De Paul University Chicago, Illinois 1998.

Beauvoir, Simone de. *All Men are Mortal*, Cleveland: World Publishing 1955.

Beauvoir, Simone de. *All Said and Done*, Harmondsworth Great Britain: Pinguin Books 1977.

Beauvoir, Simone de. *Force of Circumstance*, translated by R. Howard, Harmondsworth: Pinguin Books 1968.

Beauvoir, Simone de. *Old Age*, translated by Patrick O'Brian, Harmondsworth: Penguin Book 1978.

Beauvoir, Simone de. *Pyrrhus et Cinéas*, Paris: Gallimard 1944.

Beauvoir, Simone de. *She Came to Stay*, translated by Yvonne Moyse and Roger Senhouse, London: Fontana Paperbacks 1988.

Beauvoir, Simone de. *The Ethics of Ambiguity,* translated by Bernard Frechtman, Secaucus, N.J.: Citadel Press Book, Carol Publishing Group Edition 1997.

Beauvoir, Simone de. *The Prime of Life*, translated by P. Green, Harmondsworth: Pinguin Books 1965.

Beauvoir, Simone de. *The Second Sex,* translated by Howard M. Parshley, New York: Vintage Books Edition 1989.

Beauvoir, Simone de. "La Phénoménologie de la Perception de M. Merleau-Ponty", in: *Les Temps Modernes*, 1-2 (Nov. 1945), 363-367.

Bergoffen, Debra. *The Philosophy of Simone de Beauvoir. Gendered Phenomenologies, Erotic Generosities*, Albany: State University of New York Press 1997.

Butler, Judith. *Gender Trouble: Feminism and the Subversion of Identity,* New York & London: Routledge 1999.

Fallaize, Elizabeth (ed.). *Simone de Beauvoir: A Critical Reader,* London/New York: Routledge 1998.

Francis, Claude. Gontier, Fernande. *Les Écrits de Simone de Beauvoir*, Paris: Gallimard 1979.

Fullbrook, Kate and Edward. *Simone de Beauvoir and Jean-Paul Sartre: The Remaking of a Twentieth-Century Legend*, New York: Basic Books 1994.

Fullbrook, Kate and Edward. "Sartre's Secret Key", in: Margaret A. Simons (ed.), *Feminist Interpretations of Simone de Beauvoir*, University Park: The Pennsylvania State University Press 1995.

Heath, Jean. *She Came to Stay: The Phallus strikes back*, in: Elizabeth Fallaize (ed.), *Simone de Beauvoir. A Critical Reader*, London-New York: Routledge 1998, 171 – 182.

Heidegger, Martin. *Being and Time*, Oxford UK & Cambridge USA: Blackwell 1995.

Hegel, G.W.F.. *Philosophy of Right*, University of Chicago 1952.

Hegel, G.W.F.. *Phenomenology of Spirit,* translated by A. V. Miller, Oxford: Oxford University Press 1977.

Honneth, Axel. *Kampf um Anerkennung,* Frankfurt am Main: Suhrkamp 1994.

James, John, Helen. "The Promise of Freedom in the Thought of Simone de Beauvoir: How an Infant Smiles", in: *American Catholic Philosophical Association: Proceedings of the Annual Meeting*, 50, 1976, 72–81.

Jeanson, Francis. *Le problème moral et la pensée de Sartre*, Paris: Editions du Seuil 1947.

Kant, Immanuel. The *Critique of Judgement*, Oxford: Clarendon Press 1928.

Kruks, Sonia. "Teaching Sartre About Freedom", in: Margaret A. Simons (ed.), *Feminist Interpretations of Simone de Beauvoir*, University Park Pennsylvania State University 1995, 79-95.

Kruks, Sonia. *Retrieving Experience. Subjectivity and Recognition in Feminist Politics*, Ithaca and London: Cornell University Press 2001.

Kruks, Sonia. "Freedoms That Matter: Subjectivity and Situation in the Work of Beauvoir, Sartre, and Merleau-Ponty", in: Kruks Sonia, *Retrieving Experience. Subjectivity and Recognition in Feminist Politics*. Ithaca and London: Cornell University Press 2001, 27-51.

Kruks, Sonia. "Beauvoir: the weight of situation", in: Elizabeth Fallaize (ed.), *Simone de Beauvoir. A Critical Reader*, London and New York: Routledge 1998, 43-71.

Le Dœuff, Michèle. *Hipparchia's Choice. An Essay Concerning Women, Philosophy*, Oxford UK & Cambridge MA: Blackwell 1991.

Lundgren-Gothlin. Eva. *Sex & Existence. Simone de Beauvoir's 'The Second Sex'*, Hanover and London: Wesleyan University Press 1996.

Moi, Toril. *Simone de Beauvoir. The Making of an Intellectual Woman,* Cambridge MA: Blackwell 1994.

Moi, Toril. *What is a Woman? And Other Essays*, New York: Oxford University Press 1999.

Moi, Toril. "A Feminism of Freedom: Simone de Beauvoir", in, *What is a Woman? And Other Essays,* New York: Oxford University Press 1999.

Moser, Susanne. *Freiheit und Anerkennung bei Simone de Beauvoir*, Tübingen: edition discord 2002.

Nagl-Docekal, Herta. *Gleichbehandlung und Anerkennung von Differenz: Kontroversielle Themen feministischer politischer Philosophie*, in: *Politische Theorie. Differenz und Lebensqualität*, Nagl-Docekal, Herta und Pauer-Studer, Herlinde (Hg.), Frankfurt/M.: Suhrkamp 1996, 9-54.

O'Hagan, Timothy and Boulé. Jean-Pierre. *A Checklist of Errors in Hazel Barnes' English Translation of Jean-Paul Sartre. L'être et le néant*, British Society for Phenomenology, Norwich: UEA 1987.

Pilardi, Jo-Ann. *Feminists Read The Second Sex*, in: Margaret A. Simons (ed.), *Feminist Interpretations of Simone de Beauvoir*, University Park: The Pennsylvania State University Press 1995, 29-45.

Raynova, Yvanka B. *Liberty: The Destiny of Simone de Beauvoir*, in: *Dharshana International*, 105, January 1987, no. 1, 31-37.

Raynova, Yvanka B. *La phénoménologie des valeurs et le problème du sacrifice chez Sartre.* In : *Bulletin de la Societé Américaine de Philosophie et de Langue Française*, vol. V, Nr. 23, case 1993, 66-79.

Raynova, Yvanka B. *L'être et le néant, une lecture postpersonnaliste*, in: *Études Sartriennes*, no. 6, 1995, 79-90.

Raynova, Yvanka B. *Das andere Geschlecht im postmodernen Kontext*, in: *L'Homme. Zeitschrift für feministische Geschichtswissenschaft*, 10. Jg. Heft 1, Wien: Böhlau 1999, 79-90.

Raynova, Yvanka B. *Le deuxième sexe: Une lecture postmoderne*. In: *Le deuxième sexe: Une relecture en trois temps, 1949-1971-1999*. Sous la direction de Cécile Coderre et Marie-Blanche Tahon, Montréal : les éditions du remue-ménage 2001, p. 141.

Raynova, Yvanka B.. *Jean-Paul Sartre, A Profound Revision of Husserlian Phenomenology World Wide*, A.-T. Tyminiecka (ed.), *Analector Husserliana*, vol. 80, Dordrecht/Boston/London: Kluwer Academic Publishers 2002, 323-335.

Raynova, Yvanka B. "Für eine postmoderne Ethik der Gerechtigkeit: Simone de Beauvoir und Jean-François Lyotard, in: Yvanka B. Raynova, Susanne Moser (eds.), *Simone de Beauvoir. 50 Jahre nach dem anderen Geschlecht*, Frankfurt am Main: Peter Lang Verlag 2004, 141-155.

Sartre, Jean-Paul. *Being and Nothingness,* translated by Hazel E. Barnes. New York a.o.: Pocket Books, 1966.

Sartre, Jean-Paul. *Existentialism and Humanism,* translated by Philip Mairet, London: Methuen 1973.

Sartre, Jean Paul. *Saint Genet, Actor and Martyr*, New York: Braziller 1963.

Sartre, Jean-Paul. *Situations IX*, Paris: Gallimard 1972.

Schwarzer, Alice. *Simone de Beauvoir. Rebellin und Wegbereiterin*, Köln: Kiepenheuer & Witsch 1999.

Simons, Margaret A. *Beauvoir and The Second Sex. Feminism, Race, and the Origins of Existentialism*, Boston: Rowman & Littlefield 1999.

Simons, Margaret A. "Beauvoir's Early Philosophy: *The 1927 Diary"*, in: Margaret A. Simons, *Beauvoir and The Second Sex,* Boston: Rowman & Littlefield 1999, p. 185-245.

Simons, Margaret A. *Beauvoir Interview* (1982) in: Margaret A. Simons, *Beauvoir and the Second Sex*, Boston: Rowman & Littlefield 1999, p. 55-60.

Simons, Margaret A. "The Beginnings of Beauvoir's Existential Phenomenology", in: Wendy O'Brien and Lester Embree (ed.), *The Existential Phenomenology of Simone de Beauvoir,* Dordrecht/Boston/London: Kluwer Academic Publishers 2001, p. 17-40.

Spiegelberg, Herbert. *The Phenomenological Movement*, The Hague, Boston, London: Martinus Nijhoff Publishers 1982.

Taylor, Charles. *Source of the Self, The Making of the Modern Identity*, Harvard: Harvard University Press 1989.

Taylor, Charles. *Multiculturalism and 'The Politics of Recognition',* Princeton: Princeton University Press 1992.

Vintges, Karen. *Philosophy as Passion. The Thinking of Simone de Beauvoir*, Bloomington and Indianapolis: Indiana University Press 1996.

Ward, Julie. "Reciprocity and Friendship in Beauvoir's Thought", in: *Hypatia. A Journal of Feminist Philosophy*, Vol. 14, Bloomington: Indiana University Press 1999.

Young, Iris Marion. "Humanism, Gynocentrism and Feminist Politics ", in: *Women's Studies International Forum*, Vol. 8, Nr. 3, p. 173-183.

**Philosophie, Phänomenologie und Hermeneutik der Werte
Philosophy, Phenomenology and Hermeneutics of Values
Philosophie, Phénoménologie et Herméneutique des Valeurs**
Reihe des Instituts für Axiologische Forschungen

Herausgegeben von Yvanka B. Raynova

Band 1   Simone de Beauvoir. 50 Jahre nach dem *Anderen Geschlecht*. 2. Auflage. Herausgegeben von Yvanka B. Raynova und Susanne Moser. 2004.

Band 2   Yvanka B. Raynova / Susanne Moser (Hrsg.): Das integrale und das gebrochene Ganze. Zum 100. Geburtstag von Leo Gabriel. 2005.

Band 3   Susanne Moser: Freedom and Recognition in the Work of Simone de Beauvoir. 2008.

www.peterlang.de

Bethania Assy

Hannah Arendt – An Ethics of Personal Responsibility
Preface by Agnes Heller

Frankfurt am Main, Berlin, Bern, Bruxelles, New York, Oxford, Wien, 2008.
XXI, 191 pp.
Hannah Arendt-Studies. Edited by Antonia Grunenberg. Vol. 3
ISBN 978-3-631-54990-2 · pb. € 36.–*

Arendt understands morality not in terms of maxims or moral principles, neither in their abstract nor in their relativistic acceptation. There is an original question raised by Arendt that has not been taken seriously enough. This question has powerful moral implications, for it directs us to choose our "company among men, among things, among thoughts, in the present as well as in the past". This book is concerned with an ethics based on the visibility of our words and deeds, in which, apart our intentions, appearance is ethically relevant. In the ethics of personal responsibility stands a fundamental dimension of choice able to bridge the self and the world, consciousness and experience. This ethics takes into account three levels of responsibility: responsibility towards ourselves, or how we make our presence in the world; responsibility to judge; and responsibility to the world through the consistency of our actions.

Contents: Hannah Arendt · Ethics of Appearance · Thinking, Judging, and Willing · Responsibility · Banality of evil · Adolf Eichmann · Totalitarism · Doxa · Sensus Communis · Ethics of Exemplarity · Actor · Spectator · Promise · Forgiveness

Frankfurt am Main · Berlin · Bern · Bruxelles · New York · Oxford · Wien
Distribution: Verlag Peter Lang AG
Moosstr. 1, CH-2542 Pieterlen
Telefax 00 41 (0) 32 / 376 17 27

*The €-price includes German tax rate
Prices are subject to change without notice
Homepage http://www.peterlang.de